YOUTHNATION

YOUTHNATION

BUILDING REMARKABLE BRANDS
IN A YOUTH-DRIVEN CULTURE

MATT BRITTON

Cover image: ® Andrew Rich/Getty Images

Cover design: Christopher Ayres

This book is printed on acid-free paper.

For general information about our other products and services, please contact our Customer Care Department within the United States at (800) 762-2974, outside the United States at (317) 572-3993 or fax (317) 572-4002.

Wiley publishes in a variety of print and electronic formats and by print-on-demand. Some material included with standard print versions of this book may not be included in e-books or in print-on-demand. If this book refers to media such as a CD or DVD that is not included in the version you purchased, you may download this material at http://booksupport.wiley.com. For more information about Wiley products, visit www.wiley.com.

Library of Congress Cataloging-in-Publication Data is Available

ISBN 978-1-118-98114-6 (Hardback)
ISBN 978-1-118-98252-5 (ePDF)
ISBN 978-1-118-98253-2 (ePub)

Printed in the United States of America

10 9 8 7 6 5 4 3 2 1

This book is dedicated to my family. Without each and
every one of you pieces of me would not exist and my
thoughts and words would have less meaning.
I love you all dearly.

To my parents, Robert and Marsha
and my brothers, Evan and Joey

To my wife Elyse, son Cameron,
and daughter Ella

Contents

Foreword

The most important leadership characteristic to thrive in this ever-changing world is resilience. Resilience is the ability to fall, pick ourselves up from the floor quickly, learn, and continue with our journey. Behind resilience there is an inherent positive outlook on life based on unwavering faith in our purpose, our abilities, and the capability of the teams around us.
—Antonio Lucio

As global chief marketing and communications officer at Visa, I have been at the center of YouthNation's massive disruption to business and culture. Despite the fact that Visa, a brand of enormous scale, processes over 96 billion transactions in 200 countries during the past year, in many ways we are now forced to think and act like a nimble startup to ensure our long-term vitality.

I was deeply honored when Matt asked me to write the foreword for his first book. Matt has been an important thought partner and a key driver of change in our global organization. His electric passion for driving cultural change through social media and his deep knowledge of youth were key elements in Visa's marketing evolution.

The drivers of change below are not specific to the payments industry but have implications for businesses of all types in every corner around the world.

1. The over 2 billion smartphone users[1] around the world have forever changed the way our world communicates and consumers transact.
2. The over 3 billion Internet users around the world now have real-time access to data, tools, and content on a 24-hour news cycle, forever impacting the ways we reach and influence them.
3. The pace of innovation in the marketplace has spawned a wave of millennial-inspired startups, which have reimagined our industry.

For Visa, as for all businesses today, the way in which we manage change will determine whether we will be future leaders in our industry, or another case study of a company that has been left in the dust.

I believe that digital natives will rule the world. Whether you are a global organization with thousands of employees like Visa or a local, family-owned business, your ability to understand the principals of YouthNation is now mission critical. There is simply no way you can replace the experience of being hardwired in the new reality we live in, as today's youth are.

It is imperative, therefore, for business leaders today to empower YouthNation to directly drive change within our organizations. Only by tearing down walls and challenging legacy systems can we truly disrupt ourselves before we become disrupted into obsolescence. At Visa, we are working hard to deploy the principles of YouthNation in our brand, our products, and all of our marketing efforts—principles which you will learn about in this timely book:

1. **Put consumers at the center.** No longer can we rely on talking at consumers, but rather, we need to engage them in a conversation. We need to fully understand the needs of our various consumer segments and interact with them in ways that add value to their lives.

2. **Embrace social-at-the core.** We must design our communications with shareability in mind at every touch point. We want the consumer to feel a sense of ownership in our brand so advocacy must be earned and authentic.

3. **Everything is marketing.** Whether its the way consumers interact with our products, the way we activate global events like the World Cup or the Olympics, or the way we interact with our great merchant and banking partners, they are all reflections of Visa and must be consistent and continually deliver excellence.

I am excited to be part of this book because even as the CMO of a Fortune 500 organization, my challenges are not unique. Anyone who is looking to navigate their way to success through today's white water of change must meet the demands of disruption with the principles of YouthNation.

These are indeed challenging times, but these are also times of enormous opportunity. I am hopeful and optimistic that the impact of YouthNation on our economic and cultural landscape will bring about great innovation, impact, and ultimately advancement for America, and for the rest of the world.

Antonio Lucio is Global Chief Marketing and Communications Officer at Visa Inc. In this role, he oversees Visa's global branding, corporate relations, and marketing activities. Prior to joining Visa as CMO in December 2007, Lucio was the chief innovation and health and wellness officer for PepsiCo Inc. and, prior to that, was the senior vice president and chief marketing officer at Pepsi Cola International Beverages. Lucio has more than 25 years of global marketing and brand management experience earned at some of the world's most successful consumer packaged goods companies including Kraft General Foods, RJR Foods International, and Procter & Gamble.

Consistently recognized as one of the most active CMOs on social media, you can connect with him on Twitter @ajlucio5 and LinkedIn.

Acknowledgments

When I was growing up, I never imagined I would write a book. I mean I was the type of person that would have trouble completing an essay and many times a simple paragraph. There was one teacher I encountered growing up who taught me that writing could be a place to channel emotion and passion; Norman Walker you were that person. I will always be thankful you crossed paths with me as an impressionable youth. May you rest in peace.

It's fairly obvious that without the formation of Mr Youth (which would one day become MRY, and then spin-off CrowdTap), I would not have realized the experiences that lead to the writing of this book. I'd like to humbly acknowledge the core crew that has largely stuck by me from what feels like forever ago: Dan Lafontaine, Evan Kraut, David Weinstock, Matt Rednor, Vishal Sapra, Eric Schoenberg, and Helene Devries. I'd also like to thank the great new influences at MRY: Clare Hart, David Berkowitz, Cedric Devitt, Ian Chee, and the incredible Laura Desmond. Lastly thanks to the cronies who were with me when this journey all began; I still remember our four-person team trying to make enough noise to matter: Paul Tedeschi, Vinny Saulle, and Doug Akin. Lastly to Brandon Evans and Kareem Kouddous, your feats on CrowdTap have blown me away.

Thank you to those that took big risks on our organization and myself at various points throughout my career. From Jordan Rednor, who dove in and wrote a six-figure check, when I was still working from my Manhattan apartment, to get it all started. To Ed Razek, who gave me my first big break in 2003 in the form of a giant pink gift box in South Beach. To my Seattle friends Lisa Gurry, Tara Kriese, and Lisa Tiedt, whom for over a decade served as a constant foundational client for the agency. To Antonio Lucio, whose belief in me has helped drive MRY and my career to new levels. Lastly thank you to Carson Biederman and Tim Dibble, who decided to make an eight figure investment in Mr Youth the night before the Lehman Brothers collapse; I told you I would make you proud!

I believe whenever you achieve certain heights in your life it becomes increasingly important to sur-round yourself with others that push you to achieve more, whether they realize it or not. Throughout the writing of this book several people have inspired me, helped me, or otherwise pushed me to get this done. A big thanks goes out to friends, contemporaries, luminaries, and catalysts: Andrew Fox, Michael Lazerow, Jason Strauss, Adam Braun, Dave Kerpen, Sean Christie, Eric Hadley, Avi Savar, Elliot Bisnow, Jeff Rosenthal, Brett Leve, Jeremiah Owyang, and Ryan Schinman.

#TS: you've helped transform my body and cleanse my mind. Brooklyn for life.

This book would simply not have been possible without a dream team, which amassed seemingly overnight to help an inexperienced ADHD-saddled author actually get this thing across the finish line.

Beverly West: You have been a true partner in helping me frame and create this work. Your experience from a completely different angle of culture has given me great perspective as well as great respect for the trade of authorship. It's been a real honor, you are tremendous.

David Yarus: You are the youthful catalyst to my world. Your energy, positivity, and steady grasp on where this industry is going has kept me honest, dynamic, and inspired. I am so thankful for our relationship; the mentorship goes both ways my brother.

Chris Ayres: You will always be the best designer I've ever known. Thank you for designing the cover of this book, and the logos of MRY, Mr Youth, and CrowdTap and for being an overall incredible person.

To my MRY support team: Andrew Udin, Lianne Sheffy, Kate Bryan, Adam llenich, Glenn Grieves, Alyssa Kaiser, Toni Dawkins, and project quarterback Matt Picheny. You kept me on task and provided the needed nudge when we were falling behind.

To my assistant Brooks Credeur: you are the thread that holds it all together—*it* meaning my life. Thanks for all that you do.

To the MRY internship class of 2014—thanks for helping this book get off the ground and best of luck in your bright futures ahead: Alexandra, Christina, Collin, Danielle, Deanna, Erika, Evan, Jacob, Jessica, John, Judith, Julia, Kaitlin, Lauren, Leslie, Matar, Neha, Olyvia, Rachel, Rebecca, Rob, and Ryan.

Finally to the team at Wiley Publishing namely Elizabeth Gildea and ShannonVargo , thanks for making my first book such a great experience.

Disclosures

Throughout the writing of this book, I did my best to avoid writing about competitors of clients or otherwise biasing the content of this book with my personal interests. Although let's be honest, today everyone competes and everything is connected.

At the time of writing this book I was a shareholder in the following:

1. Publicis Groupe (owner of MRY and Mr Youth)
2. Facebook
3. Google

At the time of writing this book I was also involved in the following:

I was a major shareholder and chairman of the board at CrowdTap.

I was a member of the board of advisors at Pencils Of Promise.

I was a major shareholder and chairman of the board at Smooch Labs (owner of JSwipe).

Several current and former MRY clients at the time of writing were mentioned in this book; they are disclosed throughout where appropriate, but for an updated and full list of clients please visit www.MattBritton.com/clients.

How to Connect with Me and Learn more about YouthNation

I encourage you to reach out and connect with me to dive further into the topics discussed in this book. Below are the best ways to do so:

Twitter: This is the best way to reach me directly for one on one dialogue; response times may vary. My handle is @MattyB, or visit https://twitter.com/mattyb

Facebook: Follow this page as new topics related to the book will be updated often. Feel free to join the discussion and get involved. https://www.facebook.com/youthnation

Instagram: Follow this page for daily inspiration and new findings: http://instagram.com/youthnation

I hope you enjoy this book as much as I enjoyed writing it!

Matt Britton - @MattyB

Introduction: Forever Young

YouthNation (Yooth-nay-shun)
1. (noun): A highly influential group of over 80 million American citizens born between 1982 and 1998. They are currently aged between 18 and 34 and nearly all of them cannot remember a time when the Internet did not exist.
2. (verb): A movement of influential individuals who possess disruptive power over cultural, business, and political issues in the United States.

Youth is not just a state of mind; it's the state of the art.

YouthNation is a new phenomenon. When America itself was young, there was no youth culture to speak of. There was no place set aside for young people to discuss and share things that were of particular interest to them. In most cases, young people were never really together as a group, and as a result, had no opportunity to form a culture that was unique to them. Historically, children were at home, sequestered away from other kids their own age, and by the time they were 10 years old were expected to take their place in the adult world of work. At the beginning of America, people weren't young for very long.

In those days, the information about the world that young people received came only from adults. When they had problems or concerns, they shared it with their elders. It wasn't until very recently from a historical perspective that young people were able to spend enough time with each other, separated and apart from the worldview of adults, to find the opportunity to be youthful. Even adolescence itself is largely a twentieth-century phenomenon.

As the middle class expanded, kids began spending longer and longer periods of time in classrooms, grouped by age, outside of the influence of adults. With growing middle-class family budgets, and a burgeoning industrial economy, kids suddenly had consumer power and an identity unto themselves. As a consequence, a youth culture began to emerge, and with it a specific language and a shared appreciation for the music, literature, movies, fashion, places, ideals, and activities that spoke directly to youth, because it came directly from youth.

Suddenly, youth culture had a voice and sought out channels of communication to express that voice. Through college radio stations, self-published magazines and newsletters, grassroots movements, or homebrew computer clubs, America's youth found a way to communicate with one another, and began to establish their footprint on the culture of the adult world. But even as recently as the sixties and seventies, our nation's youth remained a fringe culture with crude tools and few resources. It was, at most, a reaction against mainstream culture that lived on the outside looking in.

Today, far from a fringe or counterculture, our nation's youth have become the driving force behind American innovation, growth, and competitive advantage globally. As a result of our technological revolution, we are now living in a YouthNation, and all the old bets are off. The power and influence of YouthNation stands to dramatically shift every business, consumer, politician, nation, city, town, and village around the world.

This epic shift is disrupting just about everything that we took for granted about the old economy:

- The importance of a college education
- The vision of the American dream
- What success actually means
- What and how we buy
- What and how we sell
- What brands must do to embrace this new national and global ethos and compete

YouthNation has broken free from the hold that big media and big advertising have had on culture, and completely transformed the approach that brands must take in order to appeal to today's target market. The ripple effect from this monumental sea of change has and will continue to completely transform the way we work, play, and live, and is demanding and encouraging us all to be, in many ways, forever young if we want to compete.

So let's be clear. For brands today, the old marketing models are over. The status quo is dead. Today's rapidly shifting marketplace requires businesses to be agile, connected, authentic, artful, meaningful, immersive, and socially responsible. In other words, today, businesses have to embody the ideals of YouthNation, regardless of age or size, in order to succeed.

In YouthNation's hyper-socialized, Instagram fanatical, experience-obsessed marketplace, youth is no longer an age, or even a demographic, but the primary catalyst of business and culture. Fortunately, thanks to technology and the progressive ideals that social media has engendered, youth has become a commodity that is available to everyone; all we have to do is figure out how to tap these new and rapidly evolving resources in our businesses, as well as in our lives.

So how do you harness the enormous power of today's youth-driven economy, where everything is changing at the pace of a teenager's attention span, and future-fit your business for long-term success?

This is the book that will give you all the tools and understanding that you will need to understand the nuances of YouthNation and harness the enormous power of the perpetual youth economy.

As the founder and CEO of MRY (formerly known as Mr Youth), an NYC-based creative and technology agency which has specialized for well over a decade in marketing to youth for such brand titans as Visa, Johnson & Johnson, and Microsoft, I've learned a lot about how YouthNation thinks, works, plays, and spends. Since I was a freshman at Boston University two decades ago handing out nightclub flyers on the corner of Kenmore Square, I've made a career out of effectively engaging YouthNation on behalf of brands, and leveraging technology in order to keep pace with the counterculture that has now become the mainstream culture itself.

From Big Data 101, which explains how to use New-Gen psychographics to market effectively in a post demographic world, to how to tell a brand story worth sharing that builds engagement and evangelism to tips for cocreating immersive and engaging experiences that build viral followings and loyal brand communities, YouthNation will offer businesses large and small an indispensible map to navigate the radically changed landscape of the present and the future marketplace.

So let's get started, and right away, because in Youth-Nation, everything happens in real time, and in the blink of a Snapchat.

1

From Status Symbol to Status Update

The notion of the status symbol goes back as far as human history. In ancient China, once a man reached 20, he was permitted to wear a cap. This was celebrated with a ceremony called *Guanli*, or Ceremony of the Cap. As each new dynasty took hold, the caste system of the cap evolved, developing ever more specific rules and privileges associated with each style. What your cap looked like, and what shape or color it was, said very important things about you. For example, in the Han Dynasty a "lowly person" had to be content wearing only a headband, whereas the elite could get really decadent and wear a headband with a matching hat.

Since its early beginnings with the highly nuanced Chinese cap trend, the notion of the status symbol really took off, taking hold all over the globe in an ever widening array of objects and styles, all designed to tell a story about the importance of the owner. In America today, Maybach vehicles, Christian Louboutin shoes, Hublot watches, and real estate in glamorous places like the Hamptons or Malibu are the de rigeur status symbols of opulence and power among the super wealthy.

America's youth has had a love/hate relationship with status symbols. For one, the glittering objects of the affluent elite have been by and large out of reach for them. In earlier generations, young people were motivated to work hard and long to reach the point where status symbols such as a beautiful home or a nice car were attainable. As the gap between aspirational youth and the affluent mainstream widened, however, the nation's youth rejected the status quo and turned to anti–status symbols to express a different kind of importance within their own cultural sphere.

Along with this shift away from traditional status symbols, came a new set of values to support this new anti-status iconography. In the sixties, for example, ripped jeans, flag t-shirts, and long hair became counter-culture status symbols. Along with these symbols came a lifestyle and world vision centered on experiences that were not about luxury but about the pure enjoyment of life in its simplest and purest form. Be-ins, happenings, and protests, became the status alternatives for a youth culture in revolt against a system that had shut them out entirely, and that stood for materialism over existentialism. For young America in those days, poverty became chic, and wealth became tacky. And so a schism grew up between the mainstream and the counterculture with regard to visions of what status really meant, what was truly important and valuable in life, and how that was expressed.

Mainstream Status Symbols in the Sixties	Counterculture Status Symbols in the Sixties
• Lincoln Continental • Travel aboard a Pan Am jet clipper • Color TV • A royal title • A suburban bungalow	• The peace sign • The Afro • Levi's • Psychedelic drugs • Tie-dyed t-shirts • Communes

The Hip-Hop Invasion and the Reimagined Status Symbol

Young America's feelings about mainstream status symbols changed dramatically in the nineties. Suddenly, traditional status symbols of luxury and affluence became more accessible to youth culture. The accessibility of luxury opened up enormous windows of opportunities for brands and entertainers alike. The emergence of hip-hop culture combined with a booming economy toward the end of the twentieth century brought status symbols to young people in a whole new way. An infinite and innovative variety of status symbols, which were accessible and available everywhere from suburban malls to urban street corners across the U.S., led a hip-hop renaissance, along with a world vision that supported this new emphasis on accessible affluence for youth.

Hip-hop status symbol highlights

Through pervasive lyrics, from the likes of Notorious B.I.G., Jay-Z, Kanye West, Mase, Nas, and others, the new importance of status symbols to young America came through loud and clear. This new youth narrative, which stressed affordable opulence, helped usher in a wave of accessible luxury goods creating status symbols in every section of the economy. Here are some of the more notable examples:

- One of the first status symbols that emerged from hip-hop's early influence was from Run DMC in 1986 by way of their hit song "My Adidas." These early rap pioneers received a multimillion dollar endorsement deal as Adidas' three-striped sneakers tread the streets from Queens to Long Beach, California, in heavy rotation.

- In 1994 Snoop Dogg donned some Tommy Hilfiger gear on *Saturday Night Live*, and sales reportedly jumped by over $90 million that year. Prior to the SNL endorsement, Tommy Hilfiger was largely an elitist fashion brand relatively unknown in inner cities and hip-hop culture.

- Leading into 2001 at least 10 Rap and R&B songs by artists including Jennifer Lopez had mentioned Cadillac's Escalade brand in their song lyrics. During the MTV video awards that year, Ludacris drove an Escalade right onto the stage. His hit song that year "Southern Hospitality" included the lyrics: "Cadillac grills, Cadillac mills, Cadillac fills." Suddenly Cadillac, which had an average consumer age of 62, had its Escalade SUV on back order in the dealerships of major cities where a whole new generation was lining up to be a reimagined Cadillac owner.

- In 2003 after Justin Timberlake wore a Von Dutch trucker hat to the Grammy after parties, stars like Britney Spears and Ashton Kutcher quickly followed suit. The Von Dutch had been in fringe existence for five years before this fortuitous set of events. After its celebrity patronage, it became a status symbol at suburban malls in white upper-middle class enclaves across America, selling out of stores at prices exceeding $100.

Through hats, cars, and sneakers, America's hip-hop and pop culture icons of the new millennium became core drivers of discretionary spending among America's youth. Logos meant more than ever before and played an increasingly important role in showcasing social status, wealth, and style, the very same way that wearing hats did in ancient China.

Logos from companies like GAP, Abercrombie & Fitch, and FUBU were brazenly branded across outerwear and considered high fashion simply because of their label. By the mid-00s, hip-hop would go on to reach arguably its cultural peak as whimsical lyrics about Gulfstream private jets, Cristal champagne, and Jacob the Jeweler bling were commonplace in songs on Casey Kasem's top 40 lists.

Status Symbols Disrupted

While much has been written about the effect of the 2008 financial collapse on American culture, its impact on pop culture and music has largely been understated. In fact a strong argument can be made that the experience of parental stress and deflated 401(k) accounts made YouthNation rethink the importance of the material status symbols that had become so important in defining their identity in the nineties.

The logos once proudly emblazoned across their chests, YouthNation realized, were nothing more than manufactured corporate symbols of a crumbling and sometimes corrupt empire. Somehow, having mom or dad splurge on a $200 pair of Air Yeezys when they were trying to piece together the monthly mortgage payment just didn't seem as cool anymore.

The foundational belief that home prices and stock values would always rise, and every generation would do better than the one before it, came crashing down with every word out of Maria Bartiromo's mouth on those scary fall 2008 mornings on CNBC. Despite the continued popularity of a select group of hip-hop artists who became bona fide crossover stars into mainstream pop (Jay-Z, Kanye West, Lil' Wayne), 2008 created a palpable shift within popular music as the once dominant genre of hip-hop gradually lost its hold on YouthNation's imagination.

A new measure of importance and a new definition of status emerged out of the social media trend that was beginning to entrance our culture. Shiny new stuff started to lose its glimmer, and in its place came a new form of status, based not on material items, but on experiences.

YouthNation's guide to creating a status symbol

Though status symbols may differ widely in form, shape, and design, there are a few key elements that all status symbols have in common. Here are the critical components that go into the creation of any breakout status symbol to guide you in the creation of your own luxury offerings:

1. **Cost:** In modern society, few things play a bigger role in establishing something as a status symbol than the amount of money it takes to acquire it. The ownership of certain things that come at great cost—a mansion, a luxury vehicle, a yacht, or vacation home—signifies economic class and, in some cases, power. In fact, the purchase of some items, such as a private jet, can propel you into an even higher social class, in this case the "jet set" which travels the world from the privacy of their own aircraft. Note: If you want to see YouthNation's take on the "jet set" follow "RichKidsOfInstagram" on Instagram (but don't procrastinate on that for too long).

   Some high-cost status symbols even seem to defy the basic principles of economics and are known as Veblen goods. The price of Veblen goods will always remain high, regardless of low demand, and in fact, lowering their cost would make them less desirable to those few with the money to burn.

2. **Exclusivity**: The more difficult something is to obtain, the more desirable it becomes as a status symbol. This is true for both goods such as the Veblen goods that defy economic principles, as well as certain services and memberships. The American Express Centurion Card, for example, is an invitation-only card made available exclusively to those who meet a set of eligibility criteria. The same applies for highly coveted nightlife establishments such as New York City's Provocateur which is widely known for only catering to the uber rich, super cool, or beautiful. For Provocateur and others like it, it's who can't get in which maintains its level of exclusivity.

3. **Identity**: Status symbols express important qualities about the identity of their owner. Ownership of expensive items and membership to exclusive clubs and services immediately mark one as wealthy, powerful, or both. But even everyday items can be imbued with powerful symbolism, especially in today's tech-obsessed culture. Early adopters of Google Glass, for example, were immediately identified as tech

elites. Owners of Mac computers are associated with creativity more often than their PC-using counterparts.

4. **Cultural significance**: Perhaps the most critical aspect of a status symbol is that it reflects the social and cultural dynamics of its time and place. For example, the tie-dyed t-shirt held little meaning before becoming popular in the late 1960s and early 1970s as a symbol of the counterculture movements taking place across the country. In the 1980s, a cordless phone signified wealth and early adoption of technology in America, but in 2015 it has become difficult to imagine using anything but a smartphone. Every status symbol is a product of its own time and place in our cultural history.

5. **Celebrity endorsement**: There is a reason why brands throw down millions of dollars for celebrities to endorse their products—it works. However, as we saw with the hip-hop movement, even when unpaid, the simple association of a product with a celebrity or culturally significant figure can cause it to go flying off of the shelves or lot. There was a 45 percent increase in consumer interest for OMEGA's Seamaster collection after it appeared on James Bond in the 2013 film, *Skyfall*. While a fictional celebrity, James Bond represents an aspirational

lifestyle that has historically held great appeal for men, and OMEGA capitalized on this association to drive sales.

The marketing around Dr. Dre's Beats by Dre brand has always relied on celebrities wearing and using the product. From Lady Gaga to Pharrell to legendary producer Dre himself, who better to recommend a pair of headphones than your favorite musician? When Apple acquired Beats for $3 billion in 2014, they were buying more than just a product but also the all-important aura of "cool" that has resulted from Beat's savvy marketing and celebrity endorsements.

From Things to Thrills

By 2010, social media had matured from a copy-based platform where status updates were predominantly shared via short-form text to a more visually based platform where status updates increasingly included images or videos. The proliferation of camera-embedded smartphones among America's youth were compelling them to take more and more photos and share what they were seeing and doing and with whomever they wanted. Consequentially, the dialogue, priorities, and the very face, literally, of social currency shifted from the accumulation of stuff to the collection of experiences. YouthNation was moving from status symbols to status updates as a measure of value and success and has never looked back.

As a result of the smartphone explosion, photos would begin to play an increasingly convenient and pervasive role in our consumption of all media. As America's youth shifted to mobile devices as a primary computing and media consumption tool, they craved shorter and shorter forms of content exclusively "designed for the flick." Since images convey emotions and experiences that short-form copy never could, the levels of engagement around images, especially within social networks, grew exponentially. It wasn't too long before brands took notice and began to build campaigns to take advantage of this new definition of status.

Bing's Summer of Doing Campaign

In 2012 Microsoft came to MRY looking to emphasize Bing's new social features, which made it easier for users to seek the opinions and advice of friends as part of the decision-making process surrounding events, purchases, travel, and more. MRY worked with Microsoft's Bing to develop a critically acclaimed campaign called "The Summer of Doing," illustrated in Figure 2.1, which focused on distributing bespoke imagery via social media with an eye toward motivating people to go out and do things with the help of Bing.

FIGURE 2.1   A social media post from the Bing "Summer of Doing" Campaign (Created by MRY)

What happened?

Every week during the summer of 2012, MRY and Bing launched a new theme and a quirky, extreme, or amazing "doing" search word, pairing it with artist-fueled imagery and a plethora of multi-platform programming. For example, during DIY-ing week, users were encouraged to hone their DIY skills and try out new projects, including home brewing and vertical gardening. Then they were encouraged to share the DIY-ing search word and imagery that had inspired them, as well as pictures of the projects they had created across their social networks.

MRY worked directly with the Bing product team so that those who searched and shared the word of the day were entered to win prizes to bring those searches to life, such as $1,000 in DIY kits and experiences.

Why it worked

The Summer of Doing encouraged people to go out and make the most of their summer with the help of Bing, transforming Microsoft's new product into an infinite variety of experiences for users that could be readily and easily shared.

By creating conversation that wasn't just *about* Bing but driving dialogue *through* Bing and its social features, sharing happened naturally. The ever-changing content and encouragement to start experiencing new things throughout the summer reinforced the idea that the new Bing was a completely fresh take on searching that encompassed experience, and as a result, the Summer of Doing campaign broke new records.

The first month of the campaign broke Bing's full year record for earned media buzz, increasing product conversation by over 60 percent and reaching over 97.5 million people. Most important, the campaign encouraged people to stop searching and get "doing." From jamming, wanderlusting, and spelunking to dubstepping, karaokeing, and celebrating, Bing helped users make the most of the 56 days of summer.

For more information about the Bing Summer of Doing campaign, check out http://mry.com/work/bing/ and http://creativeawardshowcase.com/bing/.

The Instagram Phenomenon

Given the rising predominance of images as the core of communication, it was only a matter of time before a social network broke through to serve that exact purpose. In October 2010, a former Google employee named Kevin Systrom along with college friend Mike Krieger created Instagram, a mobile application that served a simple purpose, allowing users to edit and share pictures with friends and followers.

Instagram was an instant phenomenon, first in the United States, and then around the world. By April of

2012 Instagram was reportedly downloaded more than one million times a day. Later that year, less than two years after it's inception, Facebook acquired Instagram for $1 billion dollars. The velocity of value creation from Instagram was staggering. It took a company that had only eight employees a mere two years to create a higher valuation than the *New York Times*, which had been around over 100 years.

The growth of Instagram was predicated by Youth-Nation's desire to share what they were experiencing. The photo filters built into Instagram allowed even the most mundane experience to seem beautiful, the beautiful experiences like mountaintop sunsets or mornings on the beach to look incredible, and the amateur photographer to feel and look like a true artist for the amazement of friends, family, and the world at large. Especially on platforms like Instagram, bling and brand labels just seem less interesting and less valuable than pictures of people experiencing the world. It was what you were doing rather than what you bought that would now earn you status.

Instagram helped to cement an American experience revolution, which seemed to spark from one of the worst financial collapses in our nation's history. For the first time since the sixties YouthNation was shifting away from the status symbols that defined Gen X toward a new defining trait for millennials constructed around experiences. The question du jour among millennials is "Where can I capture an unforgettable experience right now?" The constant barrage of Instagram updates from friends doing epic things is today only making the recipients yearn to do more stuff themselves. We are now in a race to collect stamps in a passport rather than cars in the garage. Today, Instagram boasts well over 300 million users worldwide, making it one of the fastest growing communication tools in history.

DIFTI (Did It for the Instagram)

As experiences continue to command an increasing importance in the identities of young and, indeed, all Americans, the pressure to experience the optimal amount has created trends that are both positive and negative.

Certainly there are many positives to be gleaned from a movement toward getting out and experiencing life. The shift away from personal consumption in the long-term can make America a more productive economy in relation to its global peers. In focusing on experiences over stuff we will likely witness a happier society as well and arguably a more sophisticated one. There are also major benefits to be derived for our environment as more items are shared and accessed versus consumed and disposed of.

There are, however, some negative impacts in line with these pressures, which need to be addressed by entertainers, teachers, parents, and businesses. I'll never forget attending a Coldplay concert recently at New York's intimate Beacon Theatre where lead vocalist Chris Martin asked the audience to put the ubiquitous smartphones away as the band debuted a song yet to be released. Coldplay specifically didn't want the song to show up in imperfect form on YouTube.

As the audience politely obeyed Martin's request, something magical happened. All the phones went away and people were actually experiencing the music and in so many ways it felt like what a live music experience was *supposed* to feel like. It is both sad and telling how stark this experience was from the phone-obsessed generation we now live in—a world where so often we are already experiencing secondhand what we are doing in the moment.

Today, due to Instagram and other platforms like it, many experiences are sought out by consumers primarily for the ability to share them with others. In many instances the motivation of the sharing is not to allow others to participate in the experience but to prove that one was actually there. Whether its cliff diving, sneaking into the DJ booth, or brushing elbows with a celebrity, for many, if it wasn't shared it never happened.

Case in point, Mission Peak in Fremont, California has a pole at the summit of its treeless peak, the top of which has proved to be a viral selfie location for millennial visitors. Apparently, unless you've climbed to the top of the pole on Mission Peak in Fremont, you really haven't lived the full Fremont experience. So today, what was once a sleepy little park that nobody thought much about, has now become a highly trafficked tourist attraction, which is clearly visible and easily accessible from two major highways.

"Some days it's like a rock concert," said Gordon Wiley, the SF Gate Regional Park Supervisor. "Ten years ago this was just a quiet little park. But now, with social media, for some reason, it's just blowing up."

Now Mission peak is plagued with overcrowding, insufficient parking, and complaints from local residents. The natural beauty of this mountain oasis has gone unchanged for countless years, but social media has changed all of that in the blink of an eye. This dynamic is replaying itself over and over: DIFTI is changing our priorities and actions.

This phenomenon is causing many to miss out on what is really happening right before their eyes because they are so busy filming it on their phones. This is not only limited to concerts but to parents who are missing the precious moments of their child's first piano recital, so they can film it and share it on Facebook (which "friends" rarely care enough about to watch anyway).

The pressure to share experience seems to be only exceeded now by the need to be validating those experiences by way of "likes." Starting as young as age 8, girls are constantly refreshing their Instagram profile with the rigor of a Fortune 500 company to see how many of their followers have liked their photo. Social validation of a personal experience can be dangerous as it can have the effect of pushing us to do more and more extreme things to gain validation from others whom we may not even really know. We are now indeed living in the experience economy. For many, the currency is the imagery and videos we've captured from our adventures rather than the meaning and substance of the experiences themselves.

#FOMO or FauxMo?

Platforms like Instagram are driving all of us to think and act younger as we spend our days watching other people live what we perceive to be better lit and more exciting lives than we do. The natural instinct, when exposed to this kind of inspiration, is to get involved or to compete. Before the social media revolution older generations never peered into what those a decade younger were doing, so they simply didn't think about it. Now we are all constantly bombarded with outrageous imagery and quite naturally, we don't want to miss out.

#FOMO, as its now referred to by YouthNation, or fear of missing out, is driving us all to seek out more extreme, youthful, bold, and exotic trips, festivals, and nightlife experiences than we would have before the age of social media came along and showed us what we were missing out on, and what we, too, could now access, just like the kids do. Burning Man, for example, which began as a radical fringe youth festival in the middle of nowhere, is now an annual event frequented by millionaires and billionaires alike who are well past the age of 40.

Just like YouthNation, we all want to feel the connectivity of being surrounded by others. In this sense, we are all, at some level, operating in the same peer-driven ecosystem as a teenager, and are perpetually hungry for bigger, better, and more shareable experiences, to give us status with friends and followers, even if the pictures we present are bigger than life, and not a truly accurate portrayal of who we are or what we are actually doing. We are increasingly allowed to live out our fantasy lives through platforms online, which is informing the way we live our actual lives in real time. This is a huge thought-grenade for brands to keep in mind as they approach their markets of today and tomorrow. Everybody, young or old, in some sense wants the very same thing: shareable and memorable life experiences that can live perpetually on social media platforms, and tell our life stories, moment by moment.

DIY: Instagram campaign

Due to its explosive popularity especially amongst YouthNation, Instagram presents a unique opportunity for brands or organizations to connect with their communities in new and interesting ways. That being said, it's also easy to lose the interest—and the follow—of your customers with just one misstep. This DIY guide will help you to master the four "pro-tips" every marketer should keep in mind when using Instagram. Getting this right means the difference between being a part of your customer's daily culture-stream versus being cut out. Let's make sure you're always insta-famous:

1. **Keep it real.** Nobody wants to see an ad on Instagram, period. Instagram is all about authenticity and telling the world what you are, as a person or as a brand, one photo at a time. Before posting, ask yourself if your photo comes off as authentic or commercialized. If it doesn't feel 100 percent real, don't post it. This isn't the channel to re-post your print ads. It's the

channel to tell your brand story authentically, the same way your customers tell and share their own stories. What does your brand care about? Where does your brand go? Who does it spend time with? The mantra of YouthNation when it comes to talking on Instagram is "show us—don't tell us."

2. **Go behind the scenes.** Too often there is a great divide between the people and processes behind products and the end-customer. Today's customer wants to get an inside look at how everything is made, the people who make it, and where everything comes from. They want to be a part of the experience. No matter what business you're in, there's a story to be told. Keep your audience engaged by giving bits and pieces of the backstory, but never too much, so they always want more. Make sure you cover everyone and everything, big and small, from the CEO all the way through to the truck driver. Think "Humans of New York" meets "National Geographic" meets "How It's Made." By giving your community a peek behind the curtain, they'll feel closer to you and your brand than any billboard—any day.

3. **Be relevant.** Follow and participate in Instagram's pop-culture social trends. From "Throwback Thursday" (#TBT) to "Man-Crush Monday" (#MCM), participating in these

cultural movements doesn't just show your audience that you're relevant and hip to the times, like they are, but also allows you to tell different stories than your day-to-day content stream. What old-school moment or memory would your customer relate to, and appreciate your brand more for loving it as well? Who does your brand crush on, and why? If there's something happening across the social web, it's better to be one of the first brands on it than one of the last. By the time the rest of the bell-curve catches up, you'll already be looking for what's next.

4. **Cross-promote.** This goes for all social media channels, not just Instagram. Wherever you find yourself in the social media landscape, the name of the game is cross-promote! Too often you'll see a brand with over a million likes on Facebook but only several thousand on Instagram. That's not okay! Share your Instagram photos across other channels to not only extend the great visual content you're producing but to encourage your fans and followers to join you on Instagram. "If you like us on Facebook, you'll love us on Instagram!" Consider running ads to your Facebook and Twitter following that drive directly to your Instagram. Make sure you've put up some quality content beforehand; you only get one chance at a first impression.

Businesses Leading the Experience Economy

As consumers continue to reprioritize their spending into the experience economy, all companies need to take notice. The expectation consumers have who stop by your business or visit your website (likely on a mobile device) is that you will wow them and create an experience that is shareworthy and remarkable.

Through my travels, I have experienced a handful of companies who truly *get it* when it comes to providing consumers with unforgettable experiences and unrivaled access as a part of the retail experience. Here are a couple of their stories.

The supermarket experience

When Whole Foods opened its first location in Brooklyn (pictured in Figure 2.2) the gentrification capital of the world, management knew it had to up the ante on the traditional retail experience to pass the bar with hyper eco–enthusiasts and skeptical hipsters. Here is how it met the challenge:

- Key to the Whole Foods strategy was giving a national brand a local flare. There are indoor displays created from the remnants of the Coney Island Boardwalk and hundreds of items stocked from

FIGURE 2.2 Whole Foods' first Brooklyn location (Licensed from Getty Images)

Brooklyn area purveyors. There is a greenhouse on the rooftop, which actually grows produce that is sold in the store.

- The location itself is used as a live stage for local artists, which includes an in-store bar and monthly gathering in connection with Arts Gowanus, a local nonprofit.

- Whole Foods lived up to its calling of being sustainable by maintaining windmills in the parking lot, which produce energy that is used in the store. In addition, Whole Foods offers on-site bicycle repair as a service to those that limit their carbon footprint traveling to the store. With experience-driven customer services like these, Whole Foods truly is walking the walk.

The nightlife experience

When investing in a night out in Las Vegas or New York, the expectations are higher than ever before. Nights out can't just deliver on a "fun time" anymore but rather have to be *Instagram worthy* and otherwise "epic." YouthNation is looking to be blown away, which is not easy to accomplish on a consistent basis.

Jason Strauss & Noah Tepperberg, proprietors of the Tao Group and long-time friends of mine, have built a hospitality empire that has perfected the art of wowing its clientele. Through an elite stable of venues, including Tao (pictured in Figure 2.3), Marquee, Lavo, and Avenue,

FIGURE 2.3 Tao Nightclub in Las Vegas (Photo by Matt Britton)

predominantly upscale patrons have experienced dining
and nightlife on steroids. In scaling a winning formula
with venues that in some cases are reaping nearly $100
million in revenue a year, Tao Group has focused on the
following:

- **Remarkable service**: Whether it's the well-dressed
  professional security guards, beautiful wait staff, or
  diligent bar staff, customers seldom waste a precious
  second wondering where their drink is or worry
  about a spilled bucket of ice. The venues seem to be
  overstaffed with trained and focused workers who
  are passionate about their jobs.

- **Shareworthy venues**: No detail is overlooked or
  spared in the design and buildout of Tao Group
  venues, which have played host to the world's top
  DJs including Kaskade, Tiesto, and David Guetta.
  The best architects, sound, and lighting experts
  dream up unrivaled environments grand and dramatic enough to embrace the experiences that are
  housed there.

- **The art of the spectacle**: Perhaps the real secret
  sauce is in the spectacles created in these venues.
  Whether it's a drone flying in from the sky to deliver
  a huge bottle of champagne (yes, that happened),
  outdoor fireworks at the peak of a blaring EDM song,
  or choreographed dancers in elaborate costumes
  flying in from the rafters, it is the spectacle that has
  become a proven method to open up the hearts,
  minds, and wallets of Jason and Noah's experience-
  obsessed and fiercely loyal consumers.

- **Celebrity validation**: The most in-demand celebrities in the world not only visit but host their birthday parties in Tao Group venues including the likes of Lebron James and Kim Kardashian. Just as celebrities validated status symbols for Gen X, they are now validating experiences for YouthNation.

The fitness experience

Physical fitness continues to make a massive resurgence in the U.S., but it's the companies that have made getting fit into an experience that are becoming the real winners. What fitness giants like Bally's (which filed for bankruptcy in 2007) failed to understand is that fitness, like so many other categories, is about the journey as much as the results. It's not just about getting in a workout and leaving, but the experience in between. Here are some major experience-infused trends affecting the fitness category:

- **Pay-as-you-go**: The transient and unpredictable schedules of YouthNation make an ongoing monthly membership cumbersome and wasteful. Hence, pay-as-you-go models embraced by successful fitness startups, including Soul Cycle and Barry's Boot Camp, emerged. With prices from $25 to $75 per class, millennials would rather overpay during active months and not pay during "down months" while having the flexibility to spontaneously invite friends who are without prohibitive membership restrictions.

- **Pushing the edges**: Fitness experiences like Tough Mudder and Spartan Race are extreme fitness events that create share-worthy experiences. Tough Mudder's *Fire In the Hole* consists of a vertical drop down a slide that takes participants though fire, while the *Electric Eel* has participants crawling through mud to avoid dangling wires that induce small electric shocks if touched. These multimedia fitness experiences can be yours starting at $375. In 2014 Tough Mudder was named one of the top 10 fastest growing companies in New York City by *Inc.* magazine.

- **Make it social**: The Color Run, pictured in Figure 2.4, now a global phenomenon, is known as

FIGURE 2.4   The Color Run event (Photo by Michele Udin)

the "happiest 5K on earth." This is not your typical run. First and foremost, Color Runs are untimed, so it's completely about the experience. Participants must wear white shirts that are then doused with cornstarch and natural food dyes, creating a colorful spectacle custom made for the age of Instagram. Runners who complete the race are treated to a dance party at the finish line sometimes featuring some of the world's top DJs.

CHAPTER 3

The Rise of Electronic Dance Music

The shift from stuff to experiences has had a profound impact on the soundtrack of YouthNation, as the popular center of gravity has seemingly shifted. Hip-hop, largely focused on messages of affluence and excess, is giving way to tech-fueled electronic dance music (EDM) largely rooted in experiences, love, and relationships—in some ways coming full circle to the sixties generation but with a much different look and sound .

The obsession with experiences and the recent explosion of EDM is driving an unprecedented proliferation of DJ-fueled outdoor festivals in the United States. In 2014 EDM festivals topped $1 billion in revenue for the first time while the EDM industry as a whole has now skyrocketed to over $6 billion in revenue. Festivals are now a rite of passage for YouthNation who willingly empties their wallets and braves the crowds with a constant finger on the Instagram trigger. What started with the Lollapalooza festival in the nineties is now an explosion of massive events creating the ultimate experiences for an audience with a thirst for bigger, brighter, and louder happenings. Below is a rundown on a few of the most popular festivals today.

Everything You Wanted to Know about Today's Festival Scene but Were Afraid to Ask

The Electronic Daisy Carnival (EDC): Occurring annually in Las Vegas, the EDM-centric Electronic Daisy Carnival, (pictured in Figure 3.1) is currently the largest festival in the U.S. In 2014, EDC Las Vegas

FIGURE 3.1 The Electronic Daisy Carnival in Las Vegas (Licensed from Getty Images)

attracted more than 400,000 attendees.[1] You read that right, EDC now hosts more people annually than attended Woodstock, an event which defined the entire sixties generation. The scale and grandeur of EDC has created a mind-blowing spectacle that has yet to be rivaled. EDC founder Pasquale Rotella has used this EDC as a flagship platform to create Insomniac, an empire that has now produced over 250 events for over 4 million attendees. Rotella was recently named the most important exec in EDM by *Rolling Stone* magazine.

Burning Man: This festival is the ultimate physical manifestation of the movement from material items to experiences. Burning Man is a week-long annual festival where a truly eclectic group gathers once a year in the Black Rock Desert to create Black Rock City, an experiment in community, art, expression, and self-reliance. This festival, which has now become a not-for-profit organization called the Burning Man Project, operates according to ten principles: radical inclusion, gifting, decommodification, radical self-reliance, radical self expression, communal effort, civic responsibility, leaving no trace, participation, and immediacy. Cash in Black Rock City is not recognized as a currency and in its place organizers encourage bartering and gifting as the primary vehicle of exchange. The climax of this event comes on the closing Saturday evening with the burning of a 40-foot wooden man as pictured in Figure 3.2. The population of Black Rock City in 2014 was over 65,000 people.[2]

Coachella: The Coachella Valley Music and Arts Festival, pictured in Figure 3.3, is a music festival held annually at the Empire Polo Club in Indio, California, just outside of Palm Springs. Coachella caters to a more affluent breed of millennials. The event's proximity to Los Angeles has created an environment that has led some to think of Coachella as a kind of Hollywoodstock. It's not uncommon at Coachella to see a group of Los Angeles runway models kicking off their high heels and dancing barefoot with flowers in their hair in order to become immersed in this experience craze. The festival's origins trace back to a 1993 concert that Pearl Jam performed at the Empire Polo Club while boycotting venues controlled by Ticketmaster. Coachella showcases popular and established musical artists, as well as emerging artists and reunited groups. In recent years EDM has

FIGURE 3.2 The Burning Man festival (Licensed from Getty Images)

taken more of a center stage at this growing festival; notable recent EDM appearances include Calvin Harris, Skrillex, Disclosure, Hardwell, and Avicii.

The list of popular festivals seems to be never ending these days: Electric Zoo, Bonnaroo, Tomorrowland, and Ultra. I wouldn't expect this craze to peak out anytime soon. The shift to experiences is not based on a moment in time or a revolution but, rather, represents a psychological shift and a restacking of the deck on what is important.

In some ways YouthNation is harkening back to the Summer of Love. In fact the rallying cry for the EDM community is "PLUR," which stands for Peace, Love, Unity, Respect. There is, however, one core difference. The intentions of this movement are as much inwardly

FIGURE 3.3 The Coachella Valley Music and Arts Festival (Licensed from Getty Images)

as outwardly focused. While Woodstock preached peace in a time of war in an effort to change government and corporate policies, YouthNation is much more focused on their pure enjoyment of the experience and finding ways to signal to others what they are about; not necessarily to change the world.

Do's and Don'ts of Festival Marketing for Brands

With festivals becoming more and more a part of mainstream culture, it's no surprise brand executives are scrambling to think of creative ways to capture and impact the festival audience. The problem is buying a booth or slapping on a sponsor logo isn't enough to attract, and can often be a turnoff for, YouthNation.

While being at a festival is a step in the right direction, it's easier for brands to miss the mark than it is to hit it, which typically means thousands (or millions) of dollars gone to waste and future experiential marketing opportunities overlooked. Successful festival marketing is all about standing out, delivering a memorable experience, and adding value. What follows is a short list of callouts and thought-starters to help plan your next concert/festival activation.

Don't be #basic

Remember, your competition isn't just the other festival sponsors, but the music itself! At a festival, there's always something happening somewhere. You're asking attendees to miss part of the festival experience to be with you—even if just for a minute. Moral of the story: Don't be ordinary or predictable. Don't be lazy. Every brand is going to have a tchotchke to give out. Think innovatively and intricately about the experience you are entering and the people you will encounter there and design your approach accordingly, or better yet, in dialogue with your target market.

A good rule of thumb is to recognize right off the bat that the first three things you think of in the festival-planning brainstorm session have already been done! In fact, the other sponsors are probably doing them right now. Great! Let them be basic. Your job is to dig deeper, collaborate more creatively, and figure out how to deliver what nobody else is even thinking about, and be remembered for your innovation and creativity.

Add value

When you're at a festival, it comes down to fundamentals. Every festivalgoer needs three things: power, water, and shade. If you can provide something attendees need, you'll have a line 24/7 and win valuable mindshare. If you can satisfy basic needs in a fun, exciting, and memorable way, you've just become their new favorite thing. This concept goes back to fundamental concepts called "need-state marketing." Figure out what your audience needs, then deliver just that, and deliver it really, really well.

Depending on the type of festival, people will have varying needs, but think ahead to how you and your brand can fill the gap and over-deliver something people don't expect or forgot to pack, and you'll be the talk of the town. It's also important to note that this should be done authentically. Duracell often sets up phone-charging stations, and CamelBak provides water-bottle refill stations. If your brand or product isn't directly applicable to the audience's day-to-day user experience, find something related that could be. If you can connect your activation to a need in YouthNation's festival routine, you become a partner and a friend, not a brand and a sponsor.

The power of word-of-mouth

Your brand presence at the festival shouldn't end at the edge of your activation footprint. Rather, think of pass-alongs and giveaways that enable festivalgoers to represent your brand in and among the crowd, back at their camp, and throughout their daily interactions. Simple examples of this are branded balloons, beach balls, and LED light-sticks. At a festival last spring Spotify blew up hundreds of three-foot green balloons (with air, not helium), and right before the drop of the headlining EDM act Steve Aoki, tossed them over the audience with everyone watching in amazement as they floated in slow-motion, overhead. Other brands give out branded flags, umbrellas, blankets, etc., so groups of friends can share the brand experience.

So ask yourself, how can your setup drive conversations among friends or even strangers? What can you give out that people will wear or use the whole day/weekend, turning them into festival brand ambassadors and walking advocates? What kind of social content can you create that lives on past the festival, becoming an artifact or souvenir of peoples' shared experience there? In a world where word-of-mouth is king, a captive audience of several thousand young, highly connected, extremely positive and open-minded individuals is a potential launching pad for greatness.

CHAPTER

4

Access over Ownership

As the experience economy takes hold, YouthNation is reshuffling the deck, moving the desire to own durable goods to the back burner. This reprioritization has sparked a revolution focused on simply accessing or renting items rather than purchasing them, including cars, electronics, tools, lodging, and even clothes. This trend stands to impact all of corporate America in a major way over the next few years and has already caused a massive disruption in the two segments where American households spend the majority of their income: automobiles and housing. The white picket fence in the burbs with a two-car garage vision of the American dream is being disrupted and transformed before our very eyes, and in record time.

- **Home Ownership:** The risk-adverse post-2008 mortgage-lending environment simply does not favor younger homebuyers, forcing many first time homeowners to rethink their housing strategies. From the 30-year period from 1983 to 2013, home ownership among 18–34 year olds has plunged nearly 20 percent.[1] At the same time, progressive upstarts have allowed consumers to access short-term rentals in practically every corner of the earth. Sitting in a home you own and working every day to pay the mortgage doesn't feel like a very thrilling experience anymore in this experience economy. The young family's destined migration to the suburbs now seems to be a thing of the past (as we will explore in future chapters) and with the skyrocketing costs of owning property in major

47

cities millennials are content to just rent and keep their options open.

- **Car Ownership:** The percentage of 16–24 year -olds with a driver's license has dropped sharply since 1997, and is now below 70 percent for the first time since 1963.[2] For those who do decide to get a driver's license, associated costs like insurance, parking, or maintenance start to really outweigh the benefits of owning a car for YouthNation. Instead a whole host of new options have arisen allowing for easy accessibility of cars only when they are needed. Further, cars are no longer the status symbols that they used to be.

The access over ownership trend is now impacting nearly every corner of our economy. "Companies must now offer rental of their products and services rather than selling them for consumption," said Jeremiah Owyang a renowned expert on the sharing economy and Founder of Crowd Companies. "This means products must be durable as they will be used by many hands. They must be able to be shared among folks. Companies may need to offer their own marketplaces."

Uber and Airbnb: the Game Changers

In a few short years, two explosive companies Airbnb and Uber, which are now verbs in the vocabulary of Youth-Nation, have grown to become tech-fueled disruptors powerful enough to permanently change the games of housing and transportation respectively. Both companies have created wildly popular and simple-to-use services, built for use on mobile devices, which have focused on disintermediation, or removing the "middle man" from the transaction. By connecting buyers and sellers directly, these upstarts have unlocked endless unused inventory and massive pent-up demand among YouthNation to access these essential services seamlessly, directly, and instantaneously.

Airbnb, was founded in 2007 by Brian Chesky and Joe Gebbia who, inspired by the need to pay their rent, turned their living room into a makeshift motel, complete with air mattresses and free breakfast (hence the "air" in the brand name). Based on the success of their mini-experiment, Brian and Joe created a platform, as pictured in Figure 4.1, that allows anyone to rent out their apartment or home directly to a tenant. Today Airbnb has become a global disruptor in the housing and lodging sectors with over half a million active listings across nearly 200 countries. No longer are travelers limited to hostels and hotels, but rather are now afforded an authentic and truly localized way to explore one of the 33,000 cities Airbnb serves.

Airbnb's impact on the hospitality industry has been profound. On any given night in a major city it is now common for more people to stay in Airbnb rooms than every other hotel in the city combined. Furthermore, a recent Boston University study revealed that for every 1 percent increase in Airbnb bookings in a given market there is a .5 percent decrease in hotel bookings.[3]

FIGURE 4.1 The Airbnb platform (Provided by Airbnb)

Yes, you read that right. Airbnb has now completely changed the game for hotel giants like Starwood and Marriott. As you might have imagined, these megachains have started to fight back and are doing so alongside local municipalities who stand to lose hundreds of millions in tax revenues not captured via traditional hotels. In late 2014 New York City's Attorney General began a massive push to shut down Airbnb's "illegal hotel listings" based on legacy state laws that in most cases prohibit tenants from renting out their apartments for stints less than 30 days.

This same story is playing itself out with taxi and limousine services through an even greater disruptor, this time to the transportation market: Uber. Founded in 2009, Uber is a company that has seemingly become an overnight economic and cultural force of nature. In early 2015, the company was valued at over $40 billion, and today counts Google as a primary investor and strategic partner, For some of you reading this, Uber is a verb, but for others (like my parents apparently) it is just another undiscovered gem compliments of YouthNation.

Uber is yet another example of how our nation's and our world's future leaders do not like talking on the phone. Before Uber, if you wanted to book a car you had to call up a dispatcher, likely set up an account, and go with an otherwise cumbersome process to reserve a car to take you to that important business meeting or airport trip. Now, reserving a car is as simple as setting up your account once, opening an app as pictured in Figure 4.2, and pressing a button. Instantly a professional driver will show up to your location and whisk you away to wherever

FIGURE 4.2   The Uber mobile application (Provided by Uber)

you want to go. When you arrive, you simply exit the car with no signatures or awkward tips—it's all just billed to your credit card.

First a luxury option for business execs seeking town cars, Uber made the natural down market expansion to include economy options in its fleet to effectively compete with taxis in major cities. Today in major cities like New York, San Francsico, and London, Uber is ubiquitous. For YouthNation, Uber has become so convenient and seamless that it has made many question the value of owning a car at all.

Like Airbnb, Uber's unforeseen success has created a swirl of controversy and sparked dozens of legal proceedings fueled by cash-starved cities and threatened taxi and limo commissions. In Washington, D.C., the President of District Cabs says they are "down 22 percent" while in Columbus, Ohio, another Uber stronghold, taxi drivers say business is down as much as 50 percent in some instances.[4]

Ultimately both Uber and Airbnb will likely win out over legacy systems, as the consumer's will trumps all.

The Uber of everything

The success of Uber has created a flurry in the startup and venture capital space, which has now come to be known as "the Uber of everything." The premise here is quite powerful: If there is an active marketplace of buyers and sellers in close proximity, it should be easy to connect them using powerful and easy to use mobile technology. It should come as no surprise that there is now an incubator called Juggernaut which exists to build "the Uber of __" applications for aspiring entrepreneurs looking to disrupt their specific industries.

Today almost every imaginable sector including food delivery, beauty, massage, and cleaning is at risk of being "Uberized." Here are just a few examples:

- **Courier Services:** Postmates offers one-hour delivery of anything in major cities.
- **Dog Watching:** DogVacay connects dog watchers with dog owners.
- **Shipping:** Just press one button, and Shyp will send someone to your house to pick up, package and ship anything at the lowest price.
- **Residential Cleaning:** Homejoy offers on-demand, in-home cleaning services.
- **Daily Office Rentals:** Sharedesk allows companies to rent out unused desks for the hour, day, week, or month.
- **Massages:** Zeel provides on-demand, in-home massages from licensed local therapists.
- **Storage:** Makespace picks up your stuff, stores it, and puts pictures of your remote closet on the cloud for easy access.

CHAPTER 5

The Communal Table

With the emergence of youth culture as the dominant engine of our society, the definition of family has taken another dramatic turn in its long and fabled American history. Today, in addition to joining together with the people we are related to by blood, the neighbors who live close by, and the institutions that we rely on for survival, YouthNation is creating families centered upon common ideals, aspirations, passions, and politics. This has brought about a whole new model of how we live, work, and collaborate with one another, and has dramatically changed how we define and whom we think of as "family."

America's youth has from its very beginnings been inclined to break away from their families of origin and create new societies around common interests and ideologies. Think of the communes of the sixties, where people came together for a cause, lived, cooked, raised their children, and provided for the common good together. These social experiments, however, remained on the fringe. The concept, though is resurfacing today in a new and reimagined way.

Today with the advent of new technologies that connect YouthNation with similar values and complimentary talents, like-minded leaders are gathering together to create pockets of innovation and cultures of creativity based on common passions and ideals in cities and towns all over America and the world. This fundamental shift is bringing about some important changes in the way our culture and the marketplace will evolve.

The De-suburbinization of America

The depiction of the American Dream as a two-car garage in the suburbs with a white picket fence has dominated our visions of family and comfort for nearly a century. The space, peace, and security of a suburban lifestyle in many ways defined the notion of success in American culture.

In recent years, however, the digital revolution has changed this vision of American utopia. We no longer need media libraries in our homes to house all of the books, VHS tapes, and compact discs which are now stored in closets and shelves in the cloud. We no longer need giant desks for our desktop computers when our televisions and computers live on our laps and in our pockets. And who needs a two-car garage when you can always just Uber?

As the lifestyles of YouthNation have become increasingly digitized, so has their "stuff" and with this massive elimination of pure clutter, the value of space and privacy has seemingly taken the backburner. The march of young professionals toward the suburbs, seeking space and tranquility when it becomes time to settle down has seemingly taken a U-turn. The rise of YouthNation is ushering in a migration back to cities in a search of ever-expanding definitions of connection and community, because there is no longer need for all of the baggage in order to feel grounded, comfortable, and connected.

The Urban Frontier

Cities have become the new frontier for millennials, evolving from a stepping-stone between college and marriage to an aspirational lifestyle destination for YouthNation resulting in a new wave of reimagined urbanization in America as illustrated in Figure 5.1.

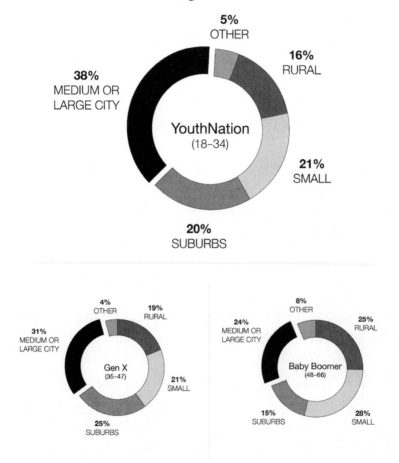

FIGURE 5.1 Where America plans to live (Created by MRY) (Source: Urban Land Institute national survey of 1,201 adults taken Jan-Feb 2013)

Why YouthNation loves cities

The migration back to cities has become a trend in Youth-
Nation because city life fits in perfectly with many of the
pillars that are driving youth culture today:

- **The shift towards experiences:** Quite simply, cities
  are where the festivals, major events, parties, and
  news occurs. YouthNation is living in their newsfeeds
  where the action is nonstop every second of every day.
  It's only natural that this constant connection to news
  about what is happening would inspire a migration
  toward the center—the source—of the action.

- **Less dependence on automobiles:** Everything is
  now just an app away. You can dry-clean your clothes
  (FlyCleaners), pick your kids up from school (Uber),
  go food shopping (Instacart), deposit a check at the
  bank (Chase), pick up a bottle of wine for dinner
  (Minibar), and more, through your phone—while
  relaxing at home. For everything else, there are
  services like eBay Now and Postmates that will
  have anything you desire delivered to your doorstep
  within the hours. In an "at your fingertips" culture
  like this, distance is not a positive; the value is in
  your proximity.

- **A move toward diversity:** YouthNation craves
  diversity and culture all around them and all
  the time, which is not generally attainable in
  homogenous suburban cul-de-sacs.

- **Cities have become a more viable long-term
  living solution:** The growing popularity of cities has

resulted in more revenue, and better city lifestyles, including reduced crime rates, improved school systems, and renewed emphasis on urban green spaces and sustainability.

Not surprisingly, Corporate America is starting to react to this urban shift. For decades our nation's largest corporations moved their headquarters out into suburbs like IBM's massive complex in suburban Armonk, New York, or Microsoft's sprawling campus in Bellevue, Washington. An attractive mixture of tax concessions, endless space, and convenience for suburban workers created massive corporate campuses that rival Central Park in scope and scale.

Now, large companies are starting to heed the gravitational pull of YouthNation toward cities, ushering in a new urban-centric era for corporate America. As of 2014, 200 of the nation's Fortune 500 companies were headquartered in one of the nation's top 50 cities.[1] Even those who haven't made the leap like General Electric and Visa are starting to dip their toes in the water with city-based innovation hubs in New York and San Francisco, respectively. The corporate towns of yesteryear, where everyone lived in the same suburb and worked for the same company, seem to be fading away.

For Fortune 500 companies to remain competitive they need to be accessible to emerging talent. As leases expire and CEO's rethink how to evolve their large institutions to compete in a digital age, it is almost certain that more buildings will shoot up in cities bearing the names of America's corporate titans.

The Youthification of Cities

As millennials settle down and have families without leaving the city, the very fabric of our population is beginning to change. The livable boundaries of major cities continue to push outward, and a new wave of youth-driven gentrification is taking hold. A common process seems to be repeating itself on the fringes of major cities across America:

- Young artists move to affordable warehousing space in the city fringes, often crime-ridden and downtrodden, where they can have room to breathe and showcase their work.

- Boutique coffee shops, vintage clothing stores, and dive bohemian venues are opened by young risk takers who can afford to be creative in their offerings and service the creative community.

- Real estate developers take note and purchase old abandoned buildings for pricey condo conversions.

- Affluent creative professionals move in as an affordable option for more space (especially those with families).

- Hip tech startups put up their flags and establish headquarters in areas that define their futuristic cultures.

- A Starbucks gets built and the original pioneers begin to get nervous.

- The locals get priced out.

- The boundaries expand even further.

DUMBO and Gowanus

One of the best-known examples of this cycle continuing to play out neighborhood by neighborhood is in Brooklyn, where a huge influx of foreign real estate investment in Manhattan has caused a mass migration across the Brooklyn Bridge especially among the city's youth. The result has been an astronomical hike in Brooklyn real estate prices in just a decade. From 2004 to 2014, real estate values in Brooklyn have increased a whopping 100 percent.[2] Now areas once considered unsafe and impoverished like Greenpoint and Bedford-Stuyvesant are looking to be the next frontier as the boundaries of livable Brooklyn expand outward. You can see this same trend occurring in the areas surrounding Jamaica Plain (extension of Boston), Wicker Park (Chicago), Wynwood (Miami), and Capitol Hill (Seattle) among others.

DUMBO, part of Brooklyn, is an acronym for the District Under Manhattan Bridge Overpass, which used to be something of a dump but has become a white-hot enclave for YouthNation of late. The moniker DUMBO arose in 1978, when residents coined it in the belief such an unattractive name would help deter developers. Young artists began moving into the area in the late 1970s and by the 1990s the area saw dramatic growth as it was cleaned up and new developments opened.

In late 2007 the neighborhood won official city status as a historic district. By that time, the Starbucks was already open, and property values were skyrocketing. Today, DUMBO is an enclave for the artists and entrepreneurs of YouthNation. Festivals, like Smorgasburg and the DUMBO Arts Festival abound, and real estate values are soaring. In 2013 DUMBO had New York City's highest concentration of technology firms by neighborhood housing 25 percent of city-based tech firms. Within a 10-block radius are 500 tech and creative firms that employ over 10,000 people.[3]

Strategically located between Park Slope (which I proudly call home), Caroll Gardens, and Cobble Hill, Gowanus is another rapidly up-and-coming neighborhood that is flourishing as a result of youthification. The area, once heavily industrialized by the Gowanus Canal, was used as a major industrial transportation route. So gas plants, paper mills, and tanneries all grew up along the Gowanus and thoroughly degraded its waters. In 2010 the Gowanus canal was added to the EPA's Superfund National Priorities List as one of the nation's most contaminated hazardous waste sites, and in 2013 the EPA finalized a plan to clean it up; the six-year plan would cost over $500 million.[4]

Hand in hand with the rejuvenation of the natural environment, the culture of Gowanus is making a triumphant resurgence. Many of the crumbling buildings that used to house now defunct plants are being rehabbed or replaced with a different kind of productivity including hotels, condos, rock climbing facilities, and arts co-ops. In 2014 the Gowanus Open Studio Tour had over 315 artists and arts organizations in the Gowanus neighborhood opening their doors to the public.[5] 2014 also saw the opening of the Royal Palms Shuffle Board

Club that has no kitchen but instead has different food truck vendors to feed the players.

As these changes take hold, the working class and blue collar populations that power major cities continue to be pushed farther and farther away from city centers as they are priced out of the neighborhoods where many of them grew up. The very notion of the "inner-city" as "a dangerous place to be avoided" is fast being replaced by "a destination of choice." Most of the places that Jay-Z raps about where he had to sell drugs growing up to survive are now surrounded by multimillion dollar condos, including those in the shadows of the sparkling new Barclays Center which now serves as home to the NBA's Brooklyn Nets which relocated from New Jersey in 2012 (thanks in part to Jay-Z himself).

The modern American Dream has evolved alongside technology. The Cleaver family ideal is over. The vision of success and tranquility that illuminated our TV screens, and the multitude of products and services that came along with that model, have been forever altered. Every company, large or small, needs to understand this fundamental shift and reshape how they go to market based on the notion that connectivity and proximity trump space and privacy.

The Peer-to-Peer Economy

Just like in the old village square where we relied on our neighbors and fellow villagers to supply what we could not provide for ourselves, we are witnessing a community-fueled renaissance of sharing among what just a decade ago would be seen as complete strangers. The urbanization of America and its newfound population density has spawned a new powerful by-product of the Internet: the peer-to-peer economy.

When eBay first exploded in the late nineties during the original Internet boom, the novelty of selling your old stuff directly to somebody else without the need for a middleman was almost too cool to pass up. The Internet's connective powers began to allow consumers from all walks of life to buy and sell anything directly to each other. A user-generated ratings system helped ensure you wouldn't get ripped off, fostering a thriving community of eBay users. Today eBay is a $60 billion company, and it stands tall among a growing graveyard of traditional retailers like Circuit City and Blockbuster Video.

Why buy a camera from a store when there is an unused one sitting in a closet 10 blocks away at a fraction of the price? Why pay for a dog sitter tonight when someone three doors down with a love for dogs and an empty calendar is willing to do it for free, or for a service you can provide in exchange? Increasingly the products and services YouthNation is looking for are coming from peers instead of businesses, and as a result an entirely different outlook for capitalism and consumption is emerging. In fact, *Fast Company* magazine estimates that the peer-to-peer economy has an estimated value of over $25 billion.[1]

The 3 P's of P2P

The peer-to-peer economy has three core pillars that sustain it, each willing and able catalysts to this disruptive movement.

Providers: Individuals with products to sell or services to offer, which can benefit others through price, convenience, accessibility, and choice

Partakers: Willing participants in the peer-to-peer economy who are buying and trading products and services

Platforms: The technologies, almost all of which are based on mobile applications, which facilitate the peer-to-peer transactions

Source: Jeremiah Owyang

Bartering Is Back

Not only has the peer-to-peer economy generated massive transactional volume between peers, but it has also created a renaissance in the bartering space. Consumers are now increasingly bartering with one another without any dollars exchanging hands. Whether its product-for-product, service-for-service, or product-for-service, the bartering space is a serious throwback to simpler times that is suddenly new and relevant again.

Yerdel, for example, is a modern day thrift shop for the peer-to-peer age. Participating users donate used durable goods to Yerdel in exchange for credits. Those credits are then used to purchase other people's used goods. We all have storage closets full of gently used stuff, and for Youth-Nation this presents the perfect opportunity to bypass traditional and costly retail channels to get their hands on the stuff that they truly want.

The Peer-to-Peer Payment Revolution

When money is actually switching hands Youth-Nation is gravitating toward a new class of payment tools that allow for quick and easy electronic transactions between individuals. Venmo, for instance, is an easy-to-use application allowing consumers to send and receive money with anyone in their phone's contact list. All you need to do is open the app, choose your recipient, and the money will appear in your recipient's Venmo account instantly. Venmo is also being embraced by YouthNation when it's time to split the bill at a restaurant or buy festival tickets.

Given the explosion of the peer-to-peer economy, companies big and small are getting into the game. Google's payments product "Google Wallet" now allows consumers to pay one another as well as for retail purchases. In late 2014, the popular messaging startup Snapchat announced the launch of Snapcash a product destined to gain traction within YouthNation. In Spring 2015 Facebook announced free peer-to-peer payment integration into its Messenger product.

The currency of trust: ratings and reviews

A critical component of the peer-to-peer economy is trust. Without it there would be a lack of governance and the floodgates for fraud and deceit would be opened. What if the person you are buying from is a fraud or the product is flawed? Originally brought to the mainstream by eBay, user ratings from both buyers and sellers have become the linchpin of trust for the peer-to-peer economy. Today, when you are finished with a ride in an Uber car, both the driver and rider are rated by each other. When you are finished with a stay at an airbnb residence, both the landlord and tenant rate each other. Over time the ratings of both buyer and seller create a trusted user identity. The more positive ratings that are received, the more confidence is built into the business transaction.

User ratings have today indeed become the FICO score of the peer-to-peer economy. If one wants to participate, one needs to earn the trust of the community, and it takes time to both build and repair your peer-to-peer credit score. Companies are also slowly starting to take notice of the importance of highly rated peer-to-peer economy providers. In late 2014, Toyota partnered with DiscoLyft, one of the most highly rated and prolific drivers on Lyft (an Uber competitor) for an advertising campaign.

Peer-to-Peer Disruption

As consumers gravitate toward one another to transact and disintermediate traditional providers, there is suddenly a lot at stake for corporate America.

As YouthNation reprioritizes their spending toward experiences and away from durable goods, the economic benefits and convenience of peer-to-peer are starting to disrupt every industry in its path. A recent study by UC Berkeley revealed that one shared car in the marketplace can result in lost auto sales of over $270,000.[2] This doesn't even take into account lost revenue in parking, loans fees, taxes, gas, etc.

The question for brands has now become "What role does my company play in the lives of youth, given that they are increasingly looking to transact with one another?" As corporate America begins to reinvent itself to compete in a YouthNation-driven marketplace with such a transformed set of priorities, it will have to grapple with the fact that its future consumers prefer access to ownership. In valuing the status update over the status symbol, the proven model of selling shiny new things at top retail rates may one day become obsolete.

Several companies of late have taken notice and successfully created partnerships or investments to integrate their business model into the peer-to-peer economy.

Peer-to-peer standout models

- In 2014 Ikea partnered with airbnb to allow consumers to stay overnight in their Sydney, Australia, location.
- Ford now offers discounts on its Explorer model to Uber and Lyft drivers and is now offering customized vehicles including built-in USB chargers.

- In 2014, eleven companies announced they were building products to integrate with Uber's API (or product platform). This allows companies like Starbucks and Hyatt to integrate directly into Uber's app for discounts and easy navigation to their locations.

While partnering with companies that are embracing peer-to-peer models certainly signals to consumers that a brand is embracing change, businesses must recognize that they are in a whole new world and disrupt themselves accordingly because YouthNation simply is not the same audience as previous generations.

The peer-to-peer economy will create opportunities for massive winners and epic losers much like the digital media transformation has forced in the past decade. Here are some examples of companies that are embracing the future.

Build it: Rent the Runway

Nestled in the second floor corridor of the red-hot Cosmopolitan Resort among traditional luxury retailers in Las Vegas is a prime location of a relatively little known Internet and brick and mortar brand called "Rent the Runway," a classic "why didn't I think of that" idea. The concept is brilliant. Searching for that perfect dress to wear out to the neighboring Marquee nightclub, women can visit a Rent the Runway retail location or online platform, pick a dress, accessorize it, and rent the whole ensemble for the night. For a fraction of the cost, shoppers can feel and look stylish for their memorable moment. There are no commitments to buy, and shoppers can use the opportunity to experiment with new styles.

This of course comes at the expense of the neighboring boutiques that traditionally have benefitted from shoppers purchasing elaborate outfits, which they would likely wear once and store in a closet forever. Rent the Runway creates a clear win/win. For the business, renting out clothing is a highly lucrative model that eliminates the traditional retail complexities of inventory management. For consumers, they are now offered an affordable and fun way to experiment with fashion at a time when they are dying to do so, without breaking the bank.

Buy it: Avis and ZipCar

Despite the fact that Avis and other major rental car companies like Hertz technically already play in the rental and sharing game, they have become victims of their dated business models as of late. The cumbersome process of renting a car, coupled with the exorbitant fee structure and inaccessible rental locations, have put them at risk in an increasingly YouthNation-driven culture and economy.

Enter ZipCar. Founded way back in 1999, ZipCar is a true innovator that saw the future of transportation long before Uber was a verb in tech circles. With hubs in 26 American cities and over one million members worldwide, ZipCar users tap into a mobile app to locate cars that are strategically parked in highly accessible city locations, which can be rented for a flat hourly fee. Using a card (no keys required), drivers can enter and start cars and drive right away. The rental fees include gas, taxes, and insurance and allow users a carefree way to access cars on a short-term basis.

Faced with an uncertain future, Avis acquired ZipCar for $500 million in 2013. In doing so, Avis went the route that Blockbuster did not when given the chance to buy Netflix. They acknowledged the tides of change in their industry and bought their way into a future model that would have likely otherwise brought about their demise.

Extend it: Coca-Cola's Wonolo

Faced with the tedious challenge of restocking shelves, coolers, displays, and vending machines and amidst a growing landscape of youth unemployment, Coca-Cola ventured outside of the beverage business to launch Wonolo. The purpose of this venture is to create short-term work opportunities by providing finite tasks within a particular locale.

For Coca-Cola, Wonolo provides an immediate business benefit in the creation of an effective tool to accomplish the arduous tasks involved in running the world's largest beverage company. On a more long-term basis, though, Coke has made the necessary step in diving into the sharing economy by extending its business to meet the needs of YouthNation head-on.

Where the Digital Meets the Physical: Meetups

The peer-to-peer economy has proven that social media, once feared to alienate people even further from one another, has, in fact, brought us closer together. While our commercial landscape has certainly been forever altered by YouthNation's community-driven renaissance, so has the way we physically meet and connect with one another. This has spawned yet another return to our heritage: the historical village town hall, only reimagined as a "meetup."

With a meetup, people are using technology to identify others within a certain radius with like-minded interests for the purposes of bringing together large spontaneous gatherings. The popularity of meetups has even spawned a thriving startup, Meetup.com, which is now one of the Top 500 most visited sites on the Internet and has counted over 100 million RSVPs[4] to local events via its service. The inspiration of Meetup.com came from co-founder Scott Heiferman who was inspired by the way New Yorkers united following the September 11th attacks. He devoted himself to deploying the Internet in a manner that made it easier to connect with strangers.

While the power of live meetings is nothing new, the soaring population density of YouthNation is now creating the ability for Meetup.com to connect those with even the most far-flung interests and hobbies to others who they can share, grow, and learn with. No longer do youth on the fringes need to feel alienated or alone. The meetups can be massive, like the NY Tech Meetup which counts over 30,000 members in its meetup community. They can also be small, like the NYC Boggle Meetup that counts 250 members who are obsessed with playing the board game Boggle. In fact in New York City there are meetup groups for owners of over 50 different dog breeds.[3]

Big brands Meetup

Like any major cultural trend, brands have been quick to jump in. Small business brand American Express Open has been a long-time supporter of meetups and has recently sponsored a Meetup.com group called "Ideas For A Growing Business," an ongoing event curriculum designed to stimulate thinking and share information and resources among small business owners.

By getting their hands dirty and adding value to those who need it most, AmEx Open stands to create lasting loyalty and advocacy among its base. Brands of all sizes will continue to use meetups as a powerful forum to bridge digital connections into real-time engagements.

In the peer-to-peer economy, all brands must realize that in order to generate growth, they must create value by forging new ways for consumers to share, connect, and transact business with one another through their products and services, and must in some ways become a conduit for a dialogue and an exchange that will happen without them.

From Meetups to hookups

Just as Meetup.com has bridged the physical and digital worlds through proximity and shared interests, a whole range of YouthNation upstarts are accomplishing the same goal—but these meetups are for a different reason: dating. The ubiquity of mobile social media has redefined dating through a range of applications making it easier and faster than ever for singles in major cities to meet.

Tinder is a mobile dating application which is clearly all the rage among YouthNation as it is rapidly approaching over 50 million users. The simplicity of Tinder is its biggest asset. Users log on to the app to see images of prospective dating candidates within a specified proximity to their current location. If a user is interested in a profile they swipe right, if they are not interested, they swipe left. If you are interested in someone that also swiped right on you, you are a match and the app connects you with one another.

For YouthNation, which is getting married later and later in life, Tinder has become something of an obsession. According to a 2014 *New York Times* report Tinder users check the app an average of 11 times a day and spend well over an hour daily perusing profiles. It should come as no surprise then, that the success of Tinder has spawned a slew of competing mobile dating apps:

Hinge: focuses on introducing you to prospects that you share Facebook friends with. What makes Hinge different is that it cuts out the creepiness of total strangers. If you have mutual friends, suitors are in a sense pre-verified, because they are coming through a network of friends that you trust, just like in the old days. Also to limit the "meat market effect" Hinge users are given 10 dating suggestions a day that they have the option to favor.

JSwipe: a product of Smooch Labs (which I serve as the Chairman of) targets the Jewish dating scene with a Tinder-like approach. Smooch Labs has plans to expand into other religious and ethnic verticals in 2015.

OKCupid: uses an expanding dataset on its users such as quizzes, ratings, and querying app activity to make dating suggestions based on a complex algorithm, rather than just showing you profiles based on proximity.

As YouthNation continues its migration into cities the ability to meet, transact, and yes, even date will become faster and easier through the power of peer-to-peer dynamics. The peer-to-peer economy is now a foundation of YouthNation lifestyle, and stands to disrupt every business in its path in the years ahead.

CHAPTER

7

The Power of the Crowd

As we have witnessed with events like the Arab Spring and more recently the Ferguson unrest, YouthNation enriched communities possess the ability to rapidly and effectively bring people together with a common interest or cause. When they do so, their reach is so profound and their impact so powerful, they can literally topple regimes that have been in power for generations.

Similarly, interactive communities sharing a common thread also have the ability to bring about more scalable global change. As high speed Internet access is now commonplace in the home in developed markets around the world, the notion of community no longer knows geographic boundaries like it did in the days of the town village square or even ten years ago.

The Staying Power of the #Hashtag

A galvanizing force in the power of the crowd is the #Hashtag. When words or phrases in social media are preceded by a pound (#) sign, this means that they are being used to identify messages on a specific topic that will be easily sorted and searched on social media sites. The #Hashtag first came into mainstream popularity via Twitter but now has extended to almost all major social media platforms including Instagram and Facebook.

The #Hashtag has made it easy for users of social media platforms to follow commentary on an issue or trend of the moment, or contribute their thoughts in a forum dedicated exclusively to a particular topic or event. When an athlete like Peyton Manning makes an amazing play in a big game, for example, it would not be uncommon for #Peyton to become a "trending topic" or one of the most talked about topics on Twitter during the game. The same goes for cultural and political issues. When protests were being formed in light of the legal decisions surrounding Mike Brown's killing in Ferguson, #Ferguson become a trending topic throughout the U.S. and allowed protest organizers to galvanize a massive movement almost instantly. #BringBackOurGirls, or #NoH8 are other such examples. And of course, after the early 2015 terrorist attack on Charlie Hebdo in Paris, #JeSuisCharlie became the global #Hashtag of the moment.

Given the popularity of #Hashtags it should come as no surprise that brands have made their fair share of attempts to hop on the train. In fact, during the 2015 Super Bowl, #Hashtags were used in 50 percent of all TV spots. The attempts to leverage #Hashtags in advertising come with serious risks though. In September of 2014 pizza brand DiGiorno sent out a tweet from its branded Twitter account that said "#WhyIStayedyouHadPizza." What the team behind the tweet did not know at the time was that #WhyIStayed had already become something of an official tagline for survivors of domestic abuse in light of the recent scandal involving NFL player Ray Rice.

As social media strengthens its grip on American culture, the #Hashtag will continue to play an increasingly important role in cutting through the chaos and bubbling up the important topics and movements of the moment, giving brands a chance to comment on a rapidly evolving culture, in real time, in conversation with their communities.

Local talent goes global

One of the most dramatic changes that virtual communities have brought about in the world and in the marketplace is that they have enabled consumers and businesses alike to harness local talent to provide goods and services that were once only available through big brand access and big brand reach. By leveraging the contributions of a large group of free agents in nearly every service industry, consumers and small businesses can now access the wisdom and talent of the crowd to source best-in-class output from literally the middle of nowhere and from every corner of the globe.

This phenomenon known as crowdsourcing has now become a legitimate and incredibly cost-effective way of doing business for even the largest of corporations and individuals alike. Whether it's getting a logo designed, hiring data entry services, gathering real-time feedback, or even sourcing advertising concepts, the wisdom and insight of the crowd can be leveraged to output incredible work with minimal expense. Crowdsourcing has given birth to a whole slew of new emerging crowdsourcing services:

iStock: IStock is a marketplace for the work of amateur photographers. Instead of paying premium license fees to a company like Getty Images, you can source and even order specific images from a crowd of over 20,000 amateur photographers. If you fancy yourself a photographer, you can join the crowd and sell your royalty-free photos to others.

99Designs: 99Designs is a community of nearly one million graphic designers. Clients of the site, ranging from local pizza shops to Adidas, host contests for the design of their websites, letterhead, logos, etc. Once the contest is posted, designers can choose to participate and submit designs for the client. A winning design is chosen, and the designer is awarded with a prize. For designers it is a great way to bid on jobs that they would normally never have access to. For the client it is an incredibly cheap way of sourcing creative services (logos start at $99).

Mechanical Turk: This Amazon.com owned platform truly leverages the scale of the crowd by allowing clients to post a Human Intelligence Task (HIT) that is essentially a task, often quite monotonous and mundane, that a computer could not accomplish. For example, you could mobilize a force of "Turkers" (there are over half a million of them) to capture a screenshot of 10,000 twitter users with the first name Otis (random example, but you get it). Other tasks include data entry of printed materials into a website or updating old prices of products from e-commerce sites every hour. It should be noted that this platform has received its fair share of criticism for being a "digital sweatshop" where workers earn as little as $2 an hour.

IdeaBounty: IdeaBounty is a platform where you can offer a cash bounty for the best idea. In a campaign for its Peparami sausage snack in the UK, globally renowned marketer Unilever fired its advertising agency only to offer a $10,000 bounty to the individual who submitted the best idea for Peperami's upcoming print and television campaign.

How Big Brands Are Stepping Up to the Plate

While the notion of crowdsourcing seems like its built for the local company or startup, Unilever is far from the only major player that is leveraging crowdsourcing techniques to create world-class advertising and communications. The strategy of crowdsourcing creative and design ideas stands to threaten the multibillion dollar advertising industry as budget-minded corporations search for ways to cut their advertising expenses, which is generally one of the largest line items on a company's expense list.

Doritos Crash the Super Bowl contest

Since 2006 Frito-Lay's Doritos brand has been trailblazing in the crowdsourcing field by leveraging the crowd for creative work on the advertising industry's largest stage: the Super Bowl. Each year Doritos tasks its fan base and the creative community at large by challenging them to create and submit handmade, homegrown 30-second TV spots, the best of which will actually run during the Super Bowl. Doritos offers bonuses of up to $1 million for selected TV spots based on their performance.

Astonishingly, during the 2010 and 2011 the Super Bowl's, Doritos consumer-made ads were ranked the #1 ads during the big game by a *USA Today* poll.[1] These are consumer-made ads competing against the works of high-powered Madison Avenue ad agencies and winning! The age of crowdsourcing is here for good.

GE's GrabCAD challenge

After designing a powerful jet engine, GE quickly realized that its brackets, at nearly five pounds each, were just too heavy to be fuel-efficient. Without the relevant internal knowledge of creating a lighter bracket using advanced manufacturing techniques, GE turned to the wisdom of the crowd.

GE found a relatively unknown Internet community called GrabCAD, consisting of over a million engineers and other specialists. Much like the 99Designs model, GE hosted a contest targeting GrabCAD members awarding $7,000 to the engineer that could design the lightest bracket capable of supporting the GE engine. After reviewing more than 1,000 entries, GE awarded the prize to a young Indonesian engineer who was able to miraculously reduce the weight of the bracket to a mere .72 pounds.[2]

The fact that this cost GE only seven thousand dollars to execute is almost as miraculous as the design of the new bracket itself, especially when you consider that GE spends billions of dollars in research and development every year to accomplish the very same sorts of tasks. The reality is that any company, even one as large as GE, can only contain so much internal expertise, and it will never match the wisdom generated from the crowd.

Crowdsourcing gone wrong: Mountain Dew's Mountain don't

As with any emerging trend, crowdsourcing is not without its risks and detractors. Creative purists from photographers to designers believe that creative crowdsourcing commoditizes an industry that practitioners look at as a specialized art form. As such, the naysayers believe that by allowing anyone to be a designer diminishes the field at large. The institutional pressure against crowdsourcing in creative industries like advertising is certainly a big reason why the success of Doritos Super Bowl efforts are not being imitated by other brands.

Perhaps the biggest risk brands face when putting their work in the hands of consumers is that consumers can be notoriously snarky and mischievous as was the case with Mountain Dew. In 2012, the soda brand turned to crowdsourcing, through a customer activation, in an effort to name its homemade green apple extension of Mountain Dew. The campaign named "Dub the Dew" was quickly hijacked by the brand's sarcastic millennial fan base. Names like "Diabeetus" and "Fapple" quickly rose to the top of the *Dub The Dew* leaderboard.

Faced with embarrassment, execs behind the promotion at parent company PepsiCo had no choice but to rapidly end the promotion. They were quick to point out the success of other Mountain Dew crowdsourced efforts including "DewMocracy," which MRY helped conceive a few years prior. The lesson here is that crowdsourcing, while innovative and cost-effective, will never completely replace the service of a seasoned professional agency. It will, however, continue to grow as a viable option for brands regardless of scale.

Crowdfunding

In addition to goods and wisdom, capital funding can also be crowdsourced. Crowdfunding is the newest sensation in the financing world and is disrupting everything from venture capital to the banking industry. Whether you are looking for a personal loan, investors to innovate a new product or business, or funds to support a cause or campaign, crowdfunding looks to have forever changed the dynamics of fundraising, investing, and borrowing.

The Kickstarter Effect

Kickstarter, founded in 2009, has grown to become the preeminent crowdfunding platform for the creative industry. Since its founding in 2009, nearly $1.5 billion has been pledged to successfully fund over 75,000 projects on this incredible platform ranging from independent films to mobile app games to music albums to technology products. Perhaps even more amazing is that nearly 8 million individuals have participated as financial backers to Kickstarter projects, and over 2 million have done so more than once.[3]

Kickstarter has proven to be an entrepreneur's dream. No longer does an aspiring artist or CEO need to rely on stodgy banks or lawyered-up venture capitalists to access desperately needed startup funds. It is truly leveling the playing field on ideas and passion and making so many great projects come to life that otherwise would likely have been dead on arrival.

How Kickstarter works

- An idea is presented to the Kickstarter community along with a total funding goal and an explanation of how the funds will be used. Ideas are often presented with product videos or other multimedia support.

- Kickstarter's community of individual backers are offered the ability to fund a range of fixed amounts and in return receive a perk related to the project if it reaches its funding goal. The perk can be a credit in a film, a sneak peek, a limited version of a product, or a signed autograph copy of an album or piece of art.

- No backers are billed until a project meets its funding goal, and Kickstarter takes a 5 percent fee of all funds raised via its platform.

Projects that Kickstarter has made possible

- **Pebble E-Paper Smartwatch:** Conceived long before Apple went to market with Apple Watch, the Pebble was one of the first viable products in the wearable technology sector. The product allowed you to seamlessly receive text messages and call notifications over your watch via a Bluetooth connection to your smartphone. Its initial funding goal was just $100,000, and it raised an eye-popping $10 Million. The Pebble's prospects are indeed dimmed significantly due to Apple's and Samsung's recent entries into the marketplace; regardless, Kickstarter helped usher in a new era of wearable technology through this project.

- **Veronica Mars:** Actress and Internet aficionado Kristen Bell successfully tapped Kickstarter to get over 90,000 backers to pledge over $5 million to fund a movie follow-up to the popular TV series *Veronica Mars*. The film, which hit theaters in 2014, received generally positive reviews despite the fact it only grossed $3.5 million in box offices worldwide. Although far from a commercial success, it was a blockbuster in the eyes of Veronica Mars's fans who funded the film in an average of $50 increments. Fans were just thrilled to see the movie get produced and could care less about its box office receipts, unlike a studio who would have seen the release as a failure.

- **The Catlow Theatre:** When the Catlow Theatre in Barrington, Illinois, was faced with shutting down its venue due to a dated theatre and poor financials, it turned to Kickstarter to keep it from fading into extinction. With a plea for help to theatre lovers everywhere, the venue was saved.

Other Crowdfunding All-Stars

Kiva.org

Kiva.org is a nonprofit platform that allows backers to lend as little as $25 to an entrepreneur in need around the world. Borrowers post profiles of their business and make use of funds for needs such as buying bundles of fishnet for a local fisherman. The borrowers agree to pay back the lenders with interest although there is no guarantee that will happen. Ironically by lending in small increments, individual lenders are able to make a big impact in ways that large banking institutions never could.

DonorsChoose.org

DonorsChoose.org is one my personal favorite crowdfunding platforms. Teachers from underfunded and underprivileged schools across the United States post requests for funding for projects that benefit their students directly. It could be a field trip, school supplies, books, or expert speakers. Unlike Kickstarter, these projects are not looking to raise millions. In some cases, just a few hundred dollars is all that's required to give a student a memorable experience.

Indiegogo

Indiegogo is another major player in the crowdfunding field, which lends itself to more personal projects that are driven by passion as opposed to profit. Everything, from art projects, to technological innovations in need of funds, to a school class raising money to buy their favorite science teacher a new Bunsen burner, can be found on Indiegogo. Indiegogo bills itself as "a way to discover projects that people are passionate about all over the world; where you can take action to help create more of what you love."

The beauty of platforms like Kiva, DonorsChoose, and Indiegogo is that lenders know exactly where their money is going. These platforms democratize the notion of help to those that are in need.

Cutting Through the Red Tape

In many ways the crowdfunding and crowdsourcing revolution has afforded the crowd a way to make its voice heard and to effect change, without going through the traditional channels of power. By appealing directly to the crowd, products, policies, and points of view are enacted purely by and for the will of the people, sometimes for the better, and sometimes for the worse.

As we have seen, appealing to a crowd can have the power to raise a mob and overthrow governments, or start scuffles in town hall meetings, preventing discussion on legislation from going forward. When the crowd is in charge, the will of the majority prevails, and those in the minority can suffer as a result. On a more positive note, crowdsourcing and crowdfunding truly are examples of pure democracy in motion, and can effect positive change rapidly that would take traditional bureaucracies years to implement.

In the Fall of 2014 Ole Miss Rebel fans stormed the field after their team upset their top-ranked rival, the Alabama Crimson Tide, and in doing so tore down both goal posts and rang up a $50,000 fine imposed by the Southeastern Conference. Before crowdfunding, the school would have been hard-pressed politically to raise the funds to pay for the fines and restitution, and likely would have had to punish the student base for its irreverence and pass on the costs to the fans. Instead, the university set up a special page on its website, where it received over $90,000 in donations from team fans in the matter of a few days. Justice was served, team spirit was preserved, and the powers that be at Ole Miss saved face. In this instance crowdfunding was a win-win for the Southeastern Conference and the Rebels alike.

Free Agency

As the peer-to–peer economy gains traction in our increasingly urban-centric culture, a more inclusive and accessible notion of entrepreneurialism has followed. With it, there is now a growing belief within YouthNation that the traditional path to creating income, which has historically been getting a job with one company and keeping that job for life, has now been forever altered. In this new peer-driven economy there is a growing independence and with it a belief in the ability for individuals to seek several different streams of income as the new foundation for a modern day career.

According to the U.S. Bureau of Labor Statistics, 36 percent of the workforce is made up of millennials and within just 10 years will account for 75 percent of the workforce.[1] As YouthNation comes to constitute the majority of working adults, their community values and belief systems, their need for flexibility, and their hard-wired grasp of technology will likely cause a dramatic shift toward a self-employed, free agency workforce. In other words, individuals won't have jobs or employers; they will have projects and clients, and those projects will be delivered at the place and time of the worker's choosing. Soon you won't need to sit next to people that annoy you or work for bosses that don't respect you. If you are talented, you will rise to the top and have a portfolio of skills that you can shop to the highest bidder.

For large companies and workers alike, this creates a win-win scenario. Saddled with legacy benefits and unsustainable overhead, the ability to tap into resources only when needed will free up corporate balance sheets to invest in future innovation. Corporate America will not need the massive space and infrastructure that is slowing it down against disruptive industry forces. It will, however, take a complete operational makeover for corporations who have become reliant upon large full-time workforces in their organizational design. The winners will be organizations that can rapidly mobilize the right forces when needed and have the ability to switch off these expenses to account for seasonality and fluctuations that affect nearly every business.

Jobs Used to Define People, Now People Define Jobs

As evidenced by my father who has successfully worked at the same law firm in Philadelphia for over 30 years and reaped the benefits of providing his family with a comfortable upper-middle class upbringing, conventional wisdom has always pointed to staying at one company for your entire career. With each step up the corporate ladder your income rose, your stature grew, and your job security strengthened,

The fact is, though, that slowly but surely we've seen a meaningful diminution of incentives for working at one company for your entire career.

Reduced pension plans or defined benefits are few and far between or unreliable, and matching 401(k)s are decreasing. Instead of staying with a job to make more money in retirement, the game may indeed now be about making as much as possible to secure your own retirement. This is further exacerbated by the idea that

YouthNation may or may not have Social Security benefits by the time they retire. In fact, over the last 25 years the portion of private wage and salaried workers participating in traditional benefits plans has been nearly cut in half; it now stands at less than 20 percent of all workers.[2]

The healthcare factor

Since the financial crisis of 2000 and continuing due to rising healthcare costs, employee-sponsored healthcare (ESH) has diminished with nearly 70 percent of healthcare costs being subsidized in 2000 compared to just 58 percent in 2012.[3] Healthcare traditionally offered a compelling reason to stay with one employer; but if you're not getting ESH, there is clearly less incentive to stay.

The introduction of Obamacare (i.e., the Patient Protection and Affordable Care Act) seems to have created even more incentive for millennials to see themselves as free agents, as now with subsidies and the extension of being a dependent until the age of 26, you can provide benefits for yourself.

With reduced corporate benefits, decreasing corporate healthcare subsidies, and a diminishing dependence on employers to provide tools and training, the attractiveness of corporate America looks to have lost its shine. YouthNation now has the power to create its own diversified opportunities for income without the hamstrings of a corporate entity. With a plethora of income options, easy access to tools and training, and a world where the next opportunity is merely a tweet away, we look to be entering a free agent society.

What has now become clear is that the YouthNation free agent movement is well under way. According to a recent independent study by the research firm Edelman Berland, there are currently an astonishing 53 million Americans conducting freelance work, over one-third of the nation's workforce. The impact of freelancers is massive, contributing $700 billion in earnings to our economy. It should not come as a surprise that it is millennials that are leading the charge with 38 percent of them freelancing—more than any other segment.[4]

The Power of LinkedIn

The impact of the professional social network LinkedIn as an accelerator of the freelance movement cannot be overstated. Launched in 2003 by preeminent Internet innovator Reid Hoffman, LinkedIn has grown to become *the* social network for the business world. When it comes to connecting with others over the social web for the purposes of career and business opportunities, LinkedIn is the only game in town. Today over 22 percent of the U.S. population visits LinkedIn every month, and that number will only rise in the years ahead.[5]

How LinkedIn works

LinkedIn has been a catalyst for the coming free agent society and provides its users with the following functionality:

- **LinkedIn professional profiles:** LinkedIn user profiles read like a modern day resume and include peer recommendations, career history, awards and accolades, portfolio samples, and courses and certifications.

- **LinkedIn professional networks:** The equivalent of your friends on Facebook or followers on Twitter are your connections. LinkedIn connections aim to be the virtual manifestation of your Rolodex. Just like in the real world, the larger your network on LinkedIn the easier it is to connect with clients who can employ you on a project-by-project basis. The hundreds of millions of profiles from professionals the world over and the massive network of professional connections have created the ultimate Swiss army knife for free agents and employees alike. Never before has the individual had so much power to access and be accessed by anyone that matters in business. If used right, LinkedIn can indeed open up a world of opportunity.

Here are the most prominent uses of LinkedIn:

- **Find anyone:** With LinkedIn's massive connected database and advanced search tools, it is now easy to find hiring and business decision makers at any company. It wasn't that long ago where you had to buy a subscription for thousands of dollars to find an often-outdated list of industry decision makers. Now it's just a search away. LinkedIn's treasure trove of data allows for pinpoint identification of anyone that matters.

- **Warm introductions:** By searching for anyone on LinkedIn you can instantly see what common connections you might have. You could have a close friend in common to a key prospect or be two to three degrees away. Once you know where the shared connections exist, you can use Linkedin's tools to create warm intriductions versus the dreaded cold call.

- **Be found:** Nearly 98 percent of recruiters use LinkedIn to find new employees and freelancers. If you want to be found for new opportunities, prioritizing your LinkedIn presence is a must. It is always shocking to me when I see students spend over $100,000 for a top-tier college degree only to "drop the ball at the goal line" with a poor LinkedIn presence.[6]

With LinkedIn everyone is now empowered to take their careers into their own hands. Individuals can market themselves like a brand and in doing so unlock opportunities that will greatly support and accelerate the freelancer movement.

Income Everywhere

The peer-to-peer economy, fueled by tools like LinkedIn, has not only made buying products and services easier for the newly urbanized YouthNation, but has also created a new twist on personal income, which is flexible, modular, and rapidly growing. If you have a skill that is in demand, there is a good chance there are endless opportunities to directly monetize that skill through the use of new technologies. The playing field for being an entrepreneur has now seemingly been leveled for anyone with a marketable skill.

TaskRabbit to the rescue

In 2008, former IBM software engineer Leah Busque was in a bind as she had run out of dog food and didn't have time to replenish her supply before going out to dinner. What should she do? Have her dog starve for the night or be late to dinner? Back then there was not a good solution to this dilemma, but today due to a company Busque founded to solve her problem, there is a solution for us all. That solution is called TaskRabbit.

TaskRabbit is a marketplace between doers (called "taskers") and buyers and earns its money by way of a 20 percent fee assessed to the taskers. Whether it's reading a book to help someone summarize it for a book club, running errands, picking up dog food, or dictating a phone call, eager taskers can tap into a network of thousands of buyers interested in procuring services as shown in Figure 8.1. Buyers on TaskRabbit post a task and are immediately connected with qualified taskers able to complete the job.

While the odd jobs procured through TaskRabbit suggest that providers lack skill or education, you might be surprised to learn that 70 percent of TaskRabbit's

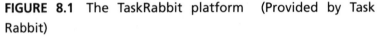

FIGURE 8.1 The TaskRabbit platform   (Provided by Task Rabbit)

providers have at least a bachelor's degree, and 20 percent have a master's degree. In other words, people with meaningful educations are turning to daily jobs to supplement income in exchange for the ability to live flexible lifestyles, free from the shackles of corporate America.

Pillars driving the free agency movement

TaskRabbit is one of many services taking advantage of the core economic principles driving the free agent movement:

- **Unused inventory:** Whether its time or stuff, we all are sitting on unused inventory. FlightCar for example allows people to rent out their cars when they are parked at the airports. Now, instead of bearing an expense for parking your car in a lot until your return, you can earn income by renting out your vehicle. If you or your stuff has downtime, there is someone that will pay for it when it is idle. Income is everywhere.

- **Vibrant marketplaces:** The ubiquity of mobile devices and their ability to sense where you are, the ease of sign-up via social networks, and the rapid adoption of new peer-to-peer services have created an abundance of vibrant marketplaces. Fiverr, which has emerged as one of the nation's Top 100 websites, offers services in creative areas like graphic design and writing for as little as $5.[7] There are now tools connecting buyers and sellers of almost everything.

- **Flexibility and convenience:** The ability to set one's own schedule allows drivers on Uber, for instance, to set their own hours around school drop-offs. In a time-shifted world where fewer and fewer of us seem to be on a 9-to-5 schedule, the free agent movement fits in hand and glove with the lifestyle choices of YouthNation.

My experience in running MRY, which now boasts over 300 employees around the world, has revealed the power and disruption of the free agency movement first-hand. What I've learned is that employees who are skilled in services that can be provided in isolated fashion are now being slowly lured into the free agency model. It is now not uncommon for ad agency creative executives to turn down salaries of over $300,000 because they can earn much more than that on a flexible basis by becoming a full-time freelancer. There is no shortage of agencies willing to pay creative directors exorbitant daily fees, and the freelance creative director has the ability to book multiple gigs at a time.

Free agency platforms

Today there are a growing roster of emerging online platforms that cater to specialists across the business world, connecting talented individual free agents with companies in need.

ODesk: the 800-pound freelance gorilla. oDesk   has grown to become a massive marketplace for freelance and niche talent. Started in 2001, oDesk, which in 2013 merged with long time competitor eLance, has grown to become a juggernaut in the freelance movement, offering the services of nearly eight million freelancers to over two million companies around the world.[8] Currently, oDesk specializes in popular areas like programming, graphic design, and search engine optimization—the number one area of expertise it offers, as illustrated in Figure 8.2. In addition, oDesk is rapidly expanding in deep niche offerings like YouTube marketing, humor writing, and infographics design.

Depth over Breadth

As platforms like oDesk and Behance (which Adobe acquired in 2012) are clearly demonstrating, there is an increasing demand for hyperspecialized skill sets. Without a growing emphasis on free agents, niche offerings like

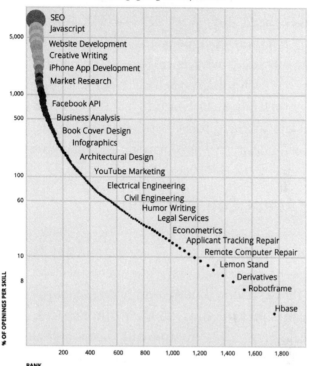

FIGURE 8.2   The long tail of skills procured on oDesk   (Provided by oDesk)

humor writing would likely have limited opportunities for full-time positions. With the ability, though, to create project work for customers that have a need for a humor writer for a finite amount of time, a funnyman can live a fruitful life by leveraging his services for dozens of companies a year and piecing together an enviable income by working for a number of clients.

As employers gain increasing abilities to leverage advanced algorithms and search tools, they no longer need to weed through candidates who are underqualified; they can find exactly the right person for the exact task they need done with a few clicks. We are moving toward a nation of hyperspecialists. No longer is it the jack-of-all-trades who is in highest demand. The complexity of technology, globalization, and disruption of nearly every industry is putting an intense focus on a deep set of skills in niche areas. In other words, instead of being an exterminator, try learning to be a squirrel exterminator.

Free Agent Collaboration

Despite the freedom and singularity of the free agency movement, we still all crave human connection. Without the offices, happy hours, and water cooler chats that companies provide through their office spaces, a lifetime of free agency has traditionally been a lonely career route. Recently though, a range of hot new startups have sprouted up to directly address the needs of free agents and entrepreneurs, providing culture, networking, and office resources that even the Googles of the world would approve of. Enter collaborative workspaces.

Originally conceived as a method to rent out desks to startup entrepreneurs, collaborative workspaces have emerged as a disruptive force in commercial real estate. In collaborative workspaces free agents and companies of all sizes rent out space by the desk or square foot for themselves or their employees. While the space they rent is exclusive to them, all other aspects of the workspace are communal including the conference rooms, the receptionist, and the coffee bar. The most poignant benefit of collaborative workspaces, though, is the networking and partnerships that are built out of the energetic environments they create.

WeWork

WeWork has created a smashing success in the collaborative workspace industry and has now expanded to 25 locations across the U.S. and houses over 2,500 businesses. In December of 2014, WeWork, which just started in 2010, was already valued at $5 billion. WeWork is built to accommodate a wide range of scenarios from an individual desk in an open environment for $350/month to over $70,000 for a space large enough to accommodate 150 workers. All members of WeWork can access a range of communal services including car rentals, healthcare plans, and even production studios. The company now has plans to expand into locations around the world including London and Tel Aviv, as the collaborative workspace phenomenon grows globally.

TechStars

TechStars has a different twist on collaborative workspaces by being built specifically for tech startups. Founded by David Cohen and Brad Feld (partner in Foundry Group, the primary investor in MRY spin-off CrowdTap), Tech-Stars serves as an incubator for promising young entrepreneurs and startups. Entrepreneurs apply to become a part of TechStars where often less than 1 percent of applicants are accepted.

Accepted applicants are provided with free office space in one of TechStars' collaborative spaces in hubs like New York, Austin, and San Francisco as well as a grant of $18,000. Each company also receives a $100,000 convertible note loan from a consortium of investors, which eventually turns into equity should the company succeed to an outside round of funding. TechStars takes a 6 percent stake in each company who joins the program.

Entrepreneurs who take part in the TechStars program have access to a group of successful entrepreneurial mentors like FourSquare founder Dennis Crowley. They also can take part in a boot camp that kicks off an intense 13-week launch program. Over 90 percent of all companies that participate in TechStars receive outside funding after graduation.[9]

TechStars has created a new way to get companies off the ground. By a communal approach, mentorship, and shared resources, entrepreneurs are given the resources they need in a shared workspace. TechStars is creating a new model for not just startups but education in general in a new world where community is paramount to success.

Eat What You Kill and the Fallacy of Detroit

As both companies and workers respond to the cultural and economic disruptions brought about by an increasingly free agent workforce, we will see a mind shift that will ultimately benefit the American economy in the long run. The notion of "eat what you kill" goes back to the dawn of humanity. Somewhere along the line, though, this driving principal of survival and success was lost in America.

Take the auto industry, for example, where strong unions and legacy benefits created overinflated workforces which during the '08 financial crisis required the federal government to bail out an entire industry. In the factories of Detroit a model was created for the American worker that was disempowering to both the employer and employee.

For the auto factories, agreements with unions and guaranteed benefits like pension programs saddled companies like General Motors and Chrysler with unsustainable cost structures and shrinking profits, which would ultimately deprive them of their ability to get ahead of new innovations like hybrid vehicles. Surely enough, competitors from Europe and Japan were able to move faster and more efficiently to push many of our fabled domestic auto institutions to the verge of extinction.

For the auto employees, there was a false sense of security provided by Big Auto. Protected by unions from being eliminated during industry fluctuations, workers believed they would always have that factory job like their mothers and fathers did the generation before. When the foreign competitors began to eat market share and the economy tanked in 2008, suddenly the jobs that were once thought of as sacred disappeared, and many of these jobs will never come back. In fact, the city of Detroit filed for bankruptcy in 2012, because it was unable to make its general debt obligations.

The lessons learned from the fall of Detroit have not been lost on YouthNation. Whether it's the medical field, legal field, or countless other professions once seen as bankable, we are now in a world where nothing is sacred, and every person must fend for themselves. This is where the true empowerment of today's generation lies.

Armed with an unprecedented arsenal of tools, technology, and access, YouthNation has the ability to create lives that previous generations would never have dreamed of. Work no longer has to be the grind that has been portrayed in movies like *Office Space*. The opportunities of this new free agent society are growing almost as quickly as the guarantees of corporate America are disappearing. Increasingly, YouthNation is taking responsibility for their future security into their own hands, likely to the benefit of us all.

CHAPTER 9

Lifehacking

Lifehacking (verb) 1. Refers to any trick, shortcut, skill, or novelty method that increases productivity and efficiency, in all walks of life. 2. A modern appropriation of a Gordian knot—anything that solves an everyday problem in an inspired, ingenious manner.

When I was growing up in my cozy suburban Lafayette Hill household just outside of Philadelphia, there was only one way, at least as far as my parents and most of my friend's parents were concerned, to be successful. Be a doctor or a lawyer, they told us. In our world, that was the only way to earn the big bucks and ensure lifelong security.

So, despite the fact I had no talent or passion for medicine or the law on any level, I just naturally assumed, when contemplating my professional future, that I would ultimately become a doctor or a lawyer. Although I had built a wildly successful nightclub promotions business during my days at Boston University, which clearly showed that my interests and skills lay elsewhere, I dutifully took the LSATs after my senior year of college because, of course, I was going to be a lawyer. In the suburbs of Philly in the nineties, there were just some things that you didn't question.

Thankfully for me and for the legal profession at large, I chose a different path. I chose passion over prudence and hacked my life, and I have never looked back. But my unusual choices have led me to think about how and why we choose our path in life, and how many more

117

choices the young people that I am surrounded by every day have when it comes to choosing theirs.

Although we consider career choice one of our inalienable rights today, in fact, choosing what you want to do when you grow up is a relatively modern idea. Two hundred years ago, what you did for a living wasn't a choice at all. If you were a woman you got married and raised a family. If you were a man, you did what your father had done. By the age of 25, you were probably already at the top of your field, or at least you had better be, because the average life expectancy in America at that time was only 35 years old.

With the advent of the industrial revolution came the birth of a more affluent middle class. Families were able to educate their children beyond the age of 9. Now the young could stay young a little longer, and have the education and the mobility to make some choices about where they wanted to live and work, and under what circumstances. A young man could now reasonably expect that if he educated himself, and then worked hard and faithfully for a company of his choosing, then he could reach the pinnacle of success and achieve wealth. A new American dream was born. Today, the traditional American corporate ideal, born out of the boom of the industrial age, doesn't really work anymore for anybody, and particularly not for YouthNation, already tempted to just opt for a lifetime of free agency.

Today, the period of preparation required to even enter the arena, the expense of that preparation, and the ever-lengthening ladder to even middle management in a global marketplace is just too daunting to contemplate. And so, young people in ever-increasing numbers are innovating their way around the long, winding, and crushingly expensive traditional roads to success, and hacking their lives. What this means for businesses today is that in order to recruit and maintain young talent, companies are coming under increasing pressure to address a completely different set of needs and expectations in order to challenge their employees to achieve their personal best and hold on to their most promising talent. The promise of gradually working your way up in a company over the course of a lifetime as a road to success, happiness, and financial gain is no longer very appealing.

Why Not Me?

For America's youth, there is now a clear disconnect between taking the established roads to success their parents took, and the new generation of success stories. Today, YouthNation is surrounded by get rich quick stories about young people, just like themselves, who elected *not* to take the long way home, but instead, hack their lives, and innovate a shortcut to success, the scale of which is often beyond any of our wildest dreams.

The feeling of "this could be me" is almost irresistible when layered against a backdrop of four years of college, awkward interviews, and what feels like a never-ending journey to the top of the corporate pyramid. In fact, the notion of higher education itself is being seriously questioned today.

Faced with student debt, stagnant wages, and unemployment, YouthNation is adopting a new attitude about higher education. A college degree no longer guarantees entrance into an oversaturated and specialized labor force.

Traditionally, enrolling in graduate school was a decision individuals made in order to distinguish themselves in the marketplace. A master's degree today, even in business administration, no longer guarantees a long-term return on investment.

In the U.S., the number of accredited business schools has outgrown demand and many programs are producing graduates that are underprepared to lead global businesses amidst a landscape that looks completely different from when they entered business school. This, coupled with the ever-growing list of business superstars who dropped out or never even attended college, is for the first time in history disrupting the idea that higher education is the only road to financial success.

11 entrepreneurs who famously never graduated from college

- Mark Zuckerberg dropped out of Harvard to start Facebook.
- David Karp dropped out of high school at 14 and founded Tumblr.
- Larry Ellison dropped out of the University of Illinois and founded Oracle.
- Michael Dell dropped out of the University of Texas and started Dell.

- Richard Branson dropped out of high school and founded Virgin.
- Russell Simmons dropped out of Manhattan City College and founded the hip-hop label DefJam.
- Steve Jobs dropped out of Reed College and founded Apple.
- Bill Gates dropped out of Harvard to found Microsoft.
- Jack Dorsey dropped out of NYU and became co-founder of Twitter and founder of Square.
- Pete Cashmore never attended college but founded Mashable at 19.
- Elon Musk dropped out of Stanford and founded Tesla.

The Internet Is the New College Campus

The traditional college model has also been greatly disrupted by the movement toward online learning. Once seen as a choice for the "strivers" of higher education via the likes of the University of Phoenix, it looks as if online education is ready to take center stage.

In 2014, Harvard and MIT, the most prestigious universities in the world, started offering online courses to millions. This, as many believe, could be a signature moment, with online education taking its place as the future shape of a college education. More specifically,

MOOCs (Massive Online Open Courses) stand to threaten the future of campus life. If the best professors in the world have the ability to lecture and test millions of students at once, then what justifies the massive expense and disruption involved with a traditional four-year education?

Currently there is over $1.2 trillion in college debt obligations shared by over 40 million Americans.[1] This burden often causes young professionals to make the wrong decisions about the jobs they take, because they are under so much pressure to satisfy their debt obligations, which is largely counterintuitive to why they attended college to begin with: to pursue their dreams.

Coupled with the rise of MOOCs is a new type of online education curriculum, which is largely peer-generated. Skillshare, for example, is an online community where anyone can master real-world skills from selected teachers who offer project-based courses online. Skill-share teachers are rated by the community and set their own prices, lengths, and locations of the courses. This democratization of education has now spread to niche areas like coding through an online learning platform called CodeAcademy.

Brand-Driven Education Models

This trend toward getting job-focused higher education over the Internet, and looking to alternative sources for life and skills training, provides a unique opportunity for brands to step into the education space, and engage, educate, and influence their future workforce from a much earlier age. Many businesses are beginning to take advantage of this opportunity including MRY.

MRY's RepNation

For students who have taken the four-year plunge, the ability to take charge of their entrepreneurial pursuits outside of the curriculum have become more important than ever before. For the last decade my own agency, MRY, has been running an initiative called RepNation. RepNation gives college students the ability to become real-life marketing representatives of Fortune 500 brands on campus. Corporate marketers such as Microsoft, Coca-Cola, Ford Motors, and Nike have all tapped into RepNation to allow students to get hands-on experience marketing major brands on campus.

For students, RepNation allows them to put away the books and really learn about the principles of sales and marketing while leveraging their innate knowledge of social media and consumer technology. For brands, it allows them to speak to young people "in their language." Tens of thousands of college students apply to be a part of RepNation every year and the fortunate participants have the ability to redefine what college education means to them.

When building MRY, I have notoriously discarded resumes as a key factor in my hiring decisions. Especially for entry-level applicants, I have often found that those with the most prestigious degrees tend to lack the street smarts to succeed at a fast-paced company. The question "What have you created?" is often the most telling way to identify those who are wired for success in today's world. Candidates who have created blogs, videos, and pieces of art, fostered movements, or participated in programs like RepNation are often the ones that have signaled the readiness and willingness to help disrupt and grow our business.

General Assembly

General Assembly was founded in January 2011 in a 20,000-square-foot loft in New York's Flatiron District by four friends in their late twenties and early thirties as a campus for technology, design, and entrepreneurship. It's not a degree-granting college; it's not a high school; it's not a traditional trade school. General Assembly is a new animal that offers augmented education—a perfect stopgap for the startup economy.

The school focuses on technology and entrepreneurship, covering everything from fundraising to wire framing. It offers specialized classes in tech, design, and entrepreneurship, and all on a flexible class schedule.

Ad agency KBSP bought classes at General Assembly in bulk as a perk for employees; the Wharton School held a daylong entrepreneurship and technology boot camp for 50 first-year students; and GE, one of the most famous names in executive education, is sending more than 100 of their executives for a five-day session that will get them up to speed on emerging technology, design, and entrepreneurship.[2]

The Innovation Imperative

If you need to be told what to do when you walk into work every day, your job will likely soon be offshored. And if you keep doing the same thing you've always done as a company, the very same thing can happen to your business. Worker or corporation, everyone must now find a way to innovate, and in order for companies to innovate they need to learn how to entice and hold on to innovators, potential free agents, and lifehackers, and make them happy within a corporate structure that these outliers might normally reject.

An often-overlooked reality is that most leaders of major corporations grew up in a world without the Internet. Their dreams were capped by the realities of the post–Industrial Revolution. Hence, their outlook on the world today and the ensuing protocols of major corporations is riddled with bureaucracy and the path most taken. This affects how big companies build their culture, make hiring decisions, and plan their futures.

It is not an understatement to say that the structure of most major corporations that fill up booths at job fairs at America's colleges are the antithesis of the life that millennials imagine for themselves. Taking a job at a major corporation is playing the long game, which is the opposite of YOLO (the YouthNation mantra of "You Only Live Once"). And at the end of the day rarely do employees working at an old-model company truly care about that new laundry detergent they are trying to sell, only how to get the next raise. This, too, is completely against the constitutional mandates of the emerging YouthNation.

Herein lies the largest problem that big business is facing when looking into the future. They know that millennials are the key to innovation and survival as every industry is now thoroughly disrupted. However, the fact is that those who are hardwired in the linear values of their pre-millennial upbringing run the majority of big businesses. The methodology of these businesses is counterintuitive to the unlimited potential that most millennials seek out for themselves. As a result, the future of America is becoming increasingly disenchanted with the notion of traditional big business and searching instead for a brazen new path toward their definition of success.

MRY's Fundamentals for Recruiting and Retaining Lifehackers

Recruiting at the entry level is an important first step in leveraging the explosive power of YouthNation. Retaining and harnessing a group obsessed with what's next provides an ongoing challenge, which should now serve as a core mandate of any CEO in order to succeed. Since creating MRY in 2002, I have been blessed with coming in contact with hundreds of incredible young professionals. For us, the path to recruiting the best and brightest has been tried and true.

MRY rules for recruiting

- Identify the best performers in our RepNation program out of the thousands of participants and hire them as summer interns (25 to 30 are hired).

- Identify the best performers in our summer internship program and offer them entry-level positions.

- Leverage our entry level staff at first to manage RepNation participants, which in turn ensures we have a continual breeding ground for young talent.

MRY rules of retention

- **Promote with rapid intuition:** The linear model of moving from a manager, to a senior manager, to an associate director, etc. is completely converse to the lifehacker mentality. I have been blessed to have the opportunity to take talented and driven people and promote them with reckless abandon. MRY execs have often found themselves in a room with folks with the same title 10 to 15 years their senior, but if they have the knowledge and confidence it doesn't matter, and they will stay and thrive.

- **Be on their level:** Creating a corporate hierarchy that extends to personalities and expectations is the quickest way to lose young talent. As an exec of a large company you can't be above sweeping the floor or playing beer pong at company outings. Don't take yourself too seriously and remember that you were once in their shoes. Creating trust and likeability among your entry-level staff creates a culture that will inspire young people to walk through fire for you.

- **Embrace intrapreneurship:** No matter how dedicated the employee, Millennials will always have some sort of "side hustle" or passion project outside of the office going on. It's part of the free agent mind-set, and should be regarded as a positive, rather than a threat. Embracing intrapreneurship in your business allows millennials who work for you to incorporate your employees' outside passions within your business structure, and as a result they will feel fulfilled while still working in a large office environment.

  Case in point, I had the good fortune of hiring Brandon Evans who started an intrapreneurship endeavor called CrowdTap, an advertising technology company, while working at MRY. With our support and funding, CrowdTap ended up growing into a full-fledged software company ranked in 2014 as one of the fastest growing private businesses in the U.S. by Inc. magazine with a three-year growth of over 5,000 percent.[3]

- **Put culture first:** Whether it's firing an abusive client or investing in a full-time in-house barista, MRY has been super-focused on creating a culture predicated on fun, spontaneity, and friendship since its inception. The company maintains an unlimited paid time off policy, has a full open seating layout in the office, and encourages employees to question the status quo. Focusing on building the right culture is table stake to embrace the true power of millennials in your business.

- **Carve out equity:** If you have a "keeper" that is set on doing their "own thing", try to carve out an equity stake for them. This will encourage them to stick around and turn the attention inward instead of outward.

- **Encourage young leaders to "break things":** All businesses need to continually encourage their future leaders to break the old systems in order to innovate new ones. A lifehacker at work "breaking" your status quo can force you to move quicker and de-corporatize from within.

- **Give mavericks their own fiefdom:** Give a lifehacker a department and a budget to operate completely and autonomously for six to nine months. Track them with a "ghost P&L" to gauge performance. See if the rest of the organization gravitates toward them or away and what success they generate.

YouthNation workplace must-haves

Looking to attract YouthNation's new breed of life-hackers to work at your company? Here are seven must-haves for your office space:

1. **In-house barista:** Caffeine is the lifeblood of most creative businesses. Why keep them running to Starbucks? This investment has paid off big-time for MRY.

2. **Unlimited PTO:** We found that when we don't count an employee's time off, they take less of it! It's a great sign of trust and translates into culture.

3. **Pet policy:** Allow pets in the office. They add a sense of calm and homliness to a work environment.

4. **Open seating plan:** It's not as loud as you think it will be and encourages continual cross-collaboration.

5. **Creative conference room names:** We once named all of our conference rooms after characters in "Mad Men"; it was great for an advertising agency.

6. **Live social wall:** Project a real-time feed of social media conversation about your employees, brand, or industry on the wall. It will make the staff feel like they have the finger on the pulse of the business.

7. **Scooters, skateboards, bikes:** Anything that allows your staff to sporadically glide through the office creates a sense of spontaneity and fun.

CHAPTER 10

The Field Guide to Lifehackers

Although lifehackers all share the same goal of pursuing a life of passion and purpose, they come in all different shapes and flavors. Here is a quick and easy reference guide to help you recognize the lifehackers that are right for your business, as well as some tips for how to recruit and motivate them to contribute their unique and innovative perspective.

The Side Hustler

Corporate Compatibility: 8

Behavior in the wild: The Side Hustler is not quite ready to take the leap into a life of free agency, yet understands there is the potential to do something more meaningful. This species of lifehacker tries to straddle both worlds and pursue their lifehack while protected by a more traditional corporate structure with its attendant security and support.

Behavior in captivity: Sneaking off to Starbucks during lunch and stealthily switching tabs to their Gmail during mid day hours is common. The side hustler always has at least one other venture in addition to work duties at all times. The end game for the side hustle, of course, is for it to be *the* hustle once it gets to a point where the risk-return makes sense.

Care and feeding: Reassure the side hustler that they can be themselves within your corporate structure. Encourage them to side hustle out in the open. Offer them the opportunity to incorporate their side hustles into their workday, as long as the work they are being paid for is prioritized. Encourage alternative and collaborative situations that allow you to benefit as a result of your support for the side hustle. Provide generous amounts of work-life balance strategies in your corporate policies that maximize the feeling of independence with support.

The definitive side hustler: Sara Blakely, founder of Spanx

Sara Blakely, history's youngest self-made female billionaire, took $5,000 in savings and turned it into a multimillion dollar women's undergarment business. After failing to make the cut for law school and being deemed too short to be a costumed Disney meet-and-greeter, 27 year old Blakely was working as a door-to-door Danka fax machine saleswoman. When she disliked the way she looked in a pair of white pants, Blakely tried traditional body-shapers but was horrified by their unflattering look and thick feel. She improvised by cutting the feet off of a pair of pantyhose but still hated how they rolled up her leg. The idea for Spanx—a flattering, functional alternative to traditional undergarments—was born.

Without any garment or fashion experience but armed with a great idea, Blakely began researching patents and cold-calling manufacturers while still maintaining her nine-to-five job. Finally, one mill owner in North Carolina decided to take a chance and help her create the product. With no money to advertise, Blakely instead took to the road to do in-store rallies with sales associates and introduce customers to Spanx. She also sent the product to Oprah's stylist. Oprah then named the product one of her favorite products of 2000, sparking $20,000 sales in less than a day and turning Spanx into a mainstream product.

Blakely has since been on the cover of *Forbes* and named #93 on their list of the world's most powerful women. Her estimated net worth is $1.1 billion while Spanx reportedly banks over $250 million in annual revenues and has net profit margins estimated at 20 percent.

The Explorer

Corporate Compatibility: 4

Behavior in the wild: The Explorer does not want to stay in one place and is obsessively pursuing a lifestyle of independence, spontaneity, and sensation. Their goal is to create a life free of the shackles of modern society. Without a home address, mortgage, cable bill, or official place of work, the Explorer lifehacker finds freedom in a life devoid of the things that many find indispensable.

Behavior in captivity: The Explorer brings a sense of adventure, a pioneering spirit, and a willingness to plunge into uncharted territories, which can be invigorating and useful to some businesses, particularly those who are pioneering new fields, technologies, or territories. In traditional settings this lifehacker can become restless, bored, or even resentful of captivity. Explorers are known to duck out early, sneak in late, or tip toe off in the middle of the day in search of stimulation and adventure.

Care and feeding: Explorers are happiest when they have control over their own schedule and have the flexibility to work remotely, so they can go anywhere they please and still meet their responsibilities. Explorers function best in businesses where travel is involved, and where a comfort level with new experiences and new locations is required.

The definitive explorer: Bear Grylls, TV host of *Man vs. Wild*, author, adventurer

Bear Grylls began his career in the British Special Air Services. After breaking his back while parachuting over Southern Africa during service he miraculously recovered to become one of the youngest people to climb Mount Everest at just 23 years old. He would then go on to write a book about it called *The Kid Who Climbed Everest*. From that point forward, Grylls became committed to breaking records and pushing limits.

Here are just a few of Grylls's record-breaking adventures:

- Hosted a dinner party at a table suspended below a hot air balloon at 24,500 feet
- Became the first person to fly over Mount Everest by powered paraglider
- Led the first unassisted crossing of the frozen North Atlantic Ocean in an inflatable boat
- Authored 15 books, including bestseller *Mud, Sweat, & Tears*, which was voted the most influential book in China for 2012
- Owns an island on the Welsh coast and lives on the River Thames on a 100 year old houseboat with his wife Shara and their sons

The Automator

Corporate Compatibility: 2

Behavior in the wild: The Automator shuns the overhead and the collateral time and resource drain of big business at every level. This lifehacker tries to break the system and finds holes to exploit where they can earn large returns through automated systems that run themselves, leaving them free to pursue passions outside of the business realm.

Behavior in captivity: Does not thrive well in a corporate setting or within the confines of a traditional work schedule. Automators place their independence above all things, and believe in accomplishing the most work in the least amount of time, and then calling it quits for the day, or the week. Automators can be of great value to businesses that wish to explore passive income sources, or streamline current operations and processes in order to create value.

Care and feeding: Offer Automators incentive-based compensation and allow them to work remotely on their own schedule in an intrapreneurial environment.

The definitive automator: Tim Ferriss, best-selling author, lifestyle designer

Tim Ferriss turned frustration stemming from his workaholic lifestyle as the CEO of a sports nutrition company into a self-help empire. Following the publication of his first book *The 4-Hour Work Week* which made the best sellers list for over four years, has been translated into 35 languages, and has sold more than 1,350,000 copies worldwide, Ferriss became renowned for the notion of the automated lifestyle. His belief is that time should be spent outside of the e-mail inbox by keeping business operations as self-regulating and self-operating as possible. Put simply, Ferris is taking the paradigm that time equals money and flipping it on its head to instead find ways to make money using the least amount of time and effort.

Ferriss, the ultimate automator, disrupted people's ideas about productivity. He reveals the secrets of how he has streamlined his business and thus freed up time for pursuits that he deemed more meaningful than work, whether that be setting a world record for the most consecutive tango spins (one of his many hobbies) or traveling the world.

The Passion Pilgrim

Corporate Compatibility: 1

Behavior in the wild: The Passion Pilgrim believes ardently in the idea of following your bliss, and lives by a credo that true success comes from a career on the intersection of passion and purpose. This lifehacker succeeds by aligning their career and daily life experience with what they love, no matter how far-flung the interest, and putting the passion for what they do above all other considerations.

Behavior in captivity: Passion Pilgrims do not generally thrive in a traditional corporate environment, as they are guided solely by their sense of purpose and interest, and don't believe in "putting in the time" unless they are passionately engaged on an almost religious basis with the company's mission and with the tasks they are involved in each day. Passion Pilgrims can be valuable to any business because of the level of commitment and investment they will deliver when and if they are authentically engaged.

Care and feeding: The Passion Pilgrim has to be inspired, infused with faith in the purpose of their mission, and constantly stimulated with work that is meaningful and immersive. Passion/purpose-based work, interest-based assignments, and specialized learning opportunities are all recommended.

The definitive passion pilgrim: Devin Graham, social media content producer

> *Ever since I was a little kid I was borrowing my parent's cameras to get the shot that no one else could. …and I have continued this passion ever since! There was never any other option; it was destiny, true love. Everyone thinks that I just go out there and have fun, party and be a rock star, but the truth of the matter is what I do, it is work; it's a crazy amount of work. I absolutely love it; I'll keep doing it 'til the day I die.*
>
> —Devin Graham

Graham's career as a videographer started as early as he could hold a camera; evolving from stop-motion Lego movies, to snowboarding films with his friends, to custom-made YouTube mega-hits for some of the biggest brands in the world, all the while staying true to his passion of telling stories and showing us the world through his eyes—and loving every second of it.

Graham's life changed when his roommate asked him to make YouTube videos for the startup he was involved with launching, the Orabrush Tooth

Cleaner. The videos instantly went viral. His use of YouTube and social media exploded the product and helped Orabrush secure distribution across every Wal-Mart in North America.

As a social media content creator and YouTube celebrity, Devin thinks of his job as a natural progression of what he's been passionate about all his life: "Honestly there's never been a transition going from this is what I love to do to this is work; it's just always been this is what I love to do." He now spends his time traveling the world filming videos he wants to shoot, now funded by big brands with big budgets, like Ford.

The Octopus

Corporate Compatibility: 5

Behavior in the wild: The Octopus is the penultimate networker who finds her way into a multitude of successful ventures. Helping herself to a piece of this and a slice of that, the Octopus has a finger in every pie, and trades connections and consulting for equity and small gigs at thriving businesses. If one of them hits, the Octopus can then roll it over into other ventures. The Octopus can be very valuable to businesses whose growth depends upon forging new and ever expanding relationships, and spotting profitable ventures or acquisitions that can generate alternate and varied sources of future value creation and new revenue streams.

Behavior in captivity: The Octopus will feel confined and will shut down if micromanaged or forced to scale down her expansive big picture perspective on the world. If given the freedom to explore her hunches, and the understanding that socializing and time spent networking outside the office are an imperative part of the job, the Octopus can be quite happy and useful in a traditional corporate setting.

Care and feeding: Macro oversight/responsibility is advised. Provide generous support and resources, and access to large volume projects at a high level. The Octopus appreciates the ability to set strategy and direction but not day-to-day.

The definitive Octopus: Rohan Oza, founder of Idea Merchants Capital

Rohan Oza is proof that you do not need to create something from scratch to be a lifehacker—instead, sometimes success is all about the ability to recognize a great idea when it comes along. A former Coca-Cola and M&M/Mars marketing executive, Oza established himself as one of the top young marketing minds well before the age of 35. After leaving Coke, Oza became a partner at Glacéau where he brought the fledgling brands VitaminWater and SmartWater to the mainstream, utilizing celebrity partnerships with notables like Lebron James, Jennifer Aniston, Kobe Bryant, and Alicia Keys as well as a lucrative endorsement and investment deal with rapper 50 Cent. As Oza put it, "They love the brand, they want to partner with the company. But they're also businesspeople. They want to invest in something they believe in."

Oza has taken this wisdom to heart when it comes to his own career trajectory and has successfully gone from a marketing star to a career mogul. Following his return to Coca-Cola as a result of the $4.1 billion purchase of Glacéau, Oza began actively investing in ideas that he loves, eventually leaving to found his own "platform for investing and building iconic brands," Idea Merchants Capital. He's since been instrumental in ensuring the success of upstart brands like Popchips, Vitacoco, Bai, Sir Kensington's Ketchup, and the wildly popular Flywheel Sports chain of spinning studios, as well as securing the investment deals from celebrities like Madonna, Rihanna, and Ashton Kutcher that put some of these brands on the map.

The Ultimate Life Hacker: Elliot Bisnow

My friend Elliot Bisnow, who like so many others dropped out of college to pursue his dreams, "hacked" his way to success by establishing a forum for young entrepreneurs like him to interact, generate ideas, and solve problems. His unwavering curiosity has redefined the notion of lifehacking by dreaming as big as one can and collaborating with other lifehackers to make this dream a reality.

In 2008, Elliot and partners Brett Leve, Jeff Rosenthal, Ryan Begelman, and Jeremy Schwartz founded the Summit Series, which began in 2008 as a three-day ski trip for 19 entrepreneurs to meet up at a pristine venue to discuss how to change the world. Elliot's ferocious networking and big vision led just a year later to President Obama asking the Summit Series team to hold a forun to discuss young entrepreneur's roles in the economic recovery.

Just a year later the momentum of the Summit Series generated a conference for 100 future leaders in Washington, D.C., which attracted elite speakers and attendees including President Clinton, Jon Legend, and Ted Turner. Then, in 2011, over 1,000 entrepreneurs including myself were fortunate enough to experience the life-changing "Summit at Sea." Over a three-day period, the Summit team managed to corral some of most influential leaders to shut off their phones and come together to tackle the world's biggest challenges. Everyone from famed entrepreneur Richard Branson to motivational speaker Sean Stephenson packed onto a chartered cruise ship. The event was groundbreaking, and inspired everyone involved to think even bigger.

Coming out of Summit at Sea, Elliot and his team set out to make Summit Series a physical place where the world's leaders and innovators could always come to achieve the inspiration of the experience at sea. So with only nominal real estate experience, they leveraged a powerful rolodex and naturally succeeded in purchasing Powder Mountain, the largest ski resort in the United States.

Summit's plans for Powder Mountain are even bolder and braver than the purchase itself. They are setting out to create a village in the beautiful mountains of Eden, Utah, inhabited by other lifehackers, leaders, philanthropists, artists, and game changers. Instead of another Aspen or the Hamptons, which are gathering places for the influential centered on opulence, Summit imagines a new belief system based on passion and purpose, rather than wealth.

Elliot Bisnow and his team have since broken ground and as of this writing have sold over 100 home sites to some of the world's leading influencers in the Summit's Eden Utah community in which they will live, work and play. They have literally made a "dent in the universe," as Steve Jobs once put it, and carved out a future which could soar as high as the mountains in Eden.

LET'S PIVOT TO BRAND BUILDING

As you have probably noticed by this point in the book, YouthNation has ushered in a cultural shift which has forever impacted the American business landscape. The belief structures of brains hardwired to the Internet through the formative years are simply worlds away from Americans of prior generations.

What really fascinates and perplexes me is the divide of those in the know and those on the outside. To think that there is still a massive portion of the U.S. population that has never heard of game changing services like Airbnb, Uber, Snapchat, or Spotify contextualizes how early we are in the YouthNation-led disruption of our nation and our world.

The influence of smartphone proliferation and their role as an extension of YouthNation's limbs is the first step of our bodies being connected to data at all times. By the time you are reading this book, Apple will have rolled out the most successful piece of wearable technology to date: the AppleWatch. We are going to be creating and accessing data faster and more efficiently than ever before.

It isn't just the human body that will be connected to devices and data. The "Internet of things" is a massive movement, which promises to have nearly every physical product connected to the Internet sending and receiving data on its performance and utility. Google's early 2014 acquisition of Nest, which produces Internet-connected thermostats, is just the beginning of a movement by tech titans to have every appliance in the home from refrigerators to toilets be connected to the Internet and getting smarter over time.

YouthNation is now in control of the success or failure of every company in every business. Whether it's a legacy industry like banking being disrupted by crowdfunding or a predominantly slow-moving industry like education being reimagined by MOOCs, business will never be the same.

This book, is about: "building brands in a youth-driven culture." Now that you understand why Youth-Nation is unlike any other generation in our history we will explore their impact on brand building in the modern age.

Despite a YouthNation-led focus on experiences over stuff, the power of brands is more relevant than ever before. Within YouthNation, brands help to form a personal identity and now, more than ever, represent culture in ways that go far beyond the products they represent. For today's entrepreneur or big-time CMO the stakes have never been higher to understand how YouthNation-driven shifts have forever changed the game in marketing and advertising. Lets dive in.

11

TV, the NFL, and the End of Demographics

The disruption that social media has created within traditional broadcast channels can be described in one word: proliferation. Today, media outlets are everywhere. They have become the opposite of the 1960s' living room where the whole country, regardless of their individual circumstances, age, or sensibilities, would gather around their living room TV sets and watch the *Ed Sullivan Show*.

In those days, reaching your target audience was much simpler because you knew where everybody would be in mass scale at any given time, based on the few shows that were broadcasting. In fact, in the dawn of television advertising, creative campaigns were merely a value-add to an industry that was focused largely on media buying as the primary commodity. Advertising under these circumstances was pretty easy: If you had a viable product, just run a spot on a top TV show. You knew everyone would watch the message, because they had no choice.

Given the vast proliferation of media channels since the sixties, you might think that finding and advertising to your target audience today would be more difficult. You may be surprised to learn, however, that by 2011, just six companies, or approximately 200 executives, controlled 90 percent of all traditional media consumed by Americans.[1] Their approach to creative content has been to keep things relatively unchanged: producing, procuring, and distributing programming capable of generating the greatest amount of consumption for the smallest investment, with the same degree of predictability for the sponsor. For media companies, the original television model works, but the problem is for advertisers, it's a different story.

The traditional TV approach to programming aims to achieve the lowest common denominator of interest levels across a broad sweeping segment of the population. These broad segments of audiences are sold to advertisers as "mass-market demographics." Niche cable networks for example, generally produce content targeting a specific subset of consumers (i.e., 18–24 year old males demographic), while broadcast networks target a wider swatch of the population (i.e., adults 18–49).

American media behemoths have benefited greatly from the creation of mass-market demographics, where for over half a century they have leveraged scale to create massive revenue windfalls. In other words, big media wins when they can chop up consumers by easily digestible, albeit rather crudely drawn subgroups, reflecting broad generalizations that could hardly meet any sort of specific point of view, or sensibility. After all, when you think about it, how is it possible to define the attitudes, tastes, and consumer characteristics of a group of individuals ranging from 18–49 years of age?

Yet, the creation of demographics, and the generic programming that targeted and captured those demographics, was designed to make media buying as easy as possible. It kept the playing field stacked for deep-pocketed advertisers who salivate over neatly packaged mass markets where they can push their commercial messages, just like in the old days with the *Ed Sullivan Show.*

During the annual TV upfronts each year (where networks like FOX and NBC present their new season's programming for advertisers to buy placement), advertisers sink an estimated $20 billion (of the $70 Billion of total TV advertising each year) into juxtaposing their commercial messages with television programming that purportedly amasses these monolithic demographics. The simplicity of mass demographics creates a safe place for advertisers to play amidst a landscape fraught with complexity growing beyond their comprehension.

The NFL's Grip on Television

Nowhere is scale achieved in a more epic way than at the annual NFL Super Bowl, the largest viewing event on broadcast television each year. The 2015 Super Bowl featuring the Seattle Seahawks and New England Patriots was the most watched television program in U.S. history with over 114 million viewers, or over one-third of all Americans tuning in.[2]

In many ways, the Super Bowl is the perfect embodiment of the days of the golden era of television, when households everywhere gathered around the same screen. The current problem with live television though, and the age-old traditional model is that with the exception of the National Football League and a few big awards shows like the Oscars and Grammys, the days of mass television audiences seem to be over.

The DVR dilemma

The successful introduction of a product called Tivo in 1999 as a commercially viable digital video recorder (DVR) became the first major disruption to the television model. Today, with DVR functionality integrated into set-top cable boxes, advertisers have grown fatigued with the impact of its rampant usage. Currently YouthNation is time-shifting 46 percent of all of their television programming according to a 2014 Comscore study.[3] If someone has time-shifted or recorded a show, they are almost undoubtedly skipping over the commercials. This has created a meaningful dilemma for the longstanding television business model.

Due to the growth of time-shifting, the resilience of the NFL as the last bastion of live television viewing has created by far the most powerful force in media. During the 2014–2015 NFL season NBC's Sunday Night Football averaged over 21 million viewers a week making it the most watched network TV show for the fifth consecutive season. Coming in at a close second, Fox's NFL Game of The Week at over 20 million viewers. These shows were not only the most watched among male viewers but female viewers alike.[4]

On top of the mass scale achieved, the NFL is almost always watched live, meaning that advertisers actually have their TV spots seen. Fully aware of its leverage, the NFL has four annual billion-dollar-plus deals with CBS, FOX, NBC, and DirecTV to broadcast its live games. However, given massive shifts in viewing habits and the deep pockets of a new breed of media

Table 11.1   The powerful ecosystems of the Big 3

	APPLE	GOOGLE	MICROSOFT
Device	iPhone	N/A	Windows Phone (Nokia)
Operating System	iOS	Android	Windows
Content Platform	iTunes	Google Play	Xbox
Search Engine/Curation	Siri	Google Search	Bing
In-Home	Apple TV	Chromecast	Xbox

Created by MRY

companies, the NFL has started to weigh its options for other partnerships that make use of nontraditional broadcasting models. What if Apple, Google, or Microsoft (which I call "the Big 3") were to shell out billions for the rights to broadcast NFL games? They all maintain complex ecosystems, shattering the capabilities of TV networks as illustrated in Table 11.1, built around the new expectations of YouthNation that include devices, operating systems, search engines, and the ability to deliver high-quality interactive content in the home.

Besides having cash coffers that dwarf those of traditional media companies, Google, Apple, and Microsoft, have the ability to serve up NFL content in a multiscreen capacity that is far more advanced and interactive than traditional media companies. They also possess ad-serving systems to create more customizable experiences for supporting brands.

It's only a matter of time before the NFL uses its massive power and influence to become the catalyst that shatters television as we know it and transforms the way we not only watch games but all TV content, ushering out the legacy system of television in the process. If this occurs, it will threaten the very existence of broadcast television networks as we understand them today.

The Big 3 possess powerful tools that allow advertisers to order pinpoint-targeted video ads the same way you order clothing from Amazon. This sweeping change will, in effect, take the mass scale of the NFL and combine it with personalization opportunities known as "addressability," which engages each viewer individually. This model could pave the way for an entirely new type of television experience, which will forever merge the television, tablet, and phone into one, synergistic media hub.

Any brand that has traditionally relied on television to reach its audience is in for a rude awakening. YouthNation has adopted habits which will soon shatter television as we know it, as soon as the NFL is ready to let it happen that is.

CHAPTER

12

Going Viral: Decoded

While traditional media companies have resisted disrupting the age old television model to keep pace with the modern consumer, the Internet continues to innovative new methods and platforms for content delivery. Today, due to social media and the endless proliferation of online channels, people have infinite choices, literally. Each individual is able to pursue their own media consumption and agendas, and to express tastes, points of view, and viewing habits that are as diverse, distinct, and unique as our population. This has changed the game completely, on and off the Super Bowl playing field.

Culture Jacking
The Dunk in the Dark Happening

In the "Mad Men" era, your success as an advertiser was limited to have a viable product and perhaps creating a great message. Today on the Internet, your message means nothing unless the right person hears it and at the right time. The art of getting your message out is now arguably more important then the message itself.

What happened?

A seminal example of social media's transformative power was seen during the infamous Super Bowl blackout of 2012 when the lights went out in the middle of the big game at the Superdome in New Orleans. With much of America amused by the confusion on their television screens and turning to their hand held screens to discuss this unexpected cultural moment, Oreo's advertising partners and executives seized the opportunity to create one of the most discussed case studies in marketing and advertising in recent memory.

The ubiquitous black-and-white cookie was already a beloved brand with American audiences, as popular among teens cruising the drugstore aisle for a snack as it is with their parents. During the year leading up to Super Bowl XLVII, Oreo had further put a stake in the ground as America's most beloved cookie by embarking on a campaign celebrating their 100th anniversary called "Daily Twist."

"Daily Twist" aimed to prove that, although a century old, the Oreo cookie was still as culturally relevant as it had ever been by reimagining pop culture moments through the lens of Oreo in real-time by way of popular social media channels like Facebook. With Oreo commenting on subjects from Gay Pride to the Mars Rover landing, this campaign not only captured the attention and acclaim of both consumers and the media but also laid the groundwork for the brand's culture-jacking of the Super Bowl.

Given the success of the "Daily Twist" campaign and their top dollar purchase of Super Bowl airtime, Oreo and their various agency partners created a Super Bowl Command Center ready to capitalize on real-time marketing opportunities during the big game. In other words, if something unexpected happened during the big game, Oreo wanted to be set up to capitalize on it. So when the lights went out in the Superdome, research revealed that a huge number of the 110+ million Super Bowl viewers were taking to social media during the lapse in game-play, creating the perfect opportunity for Oreo to reach an action-starved audience.

Since all of the key brand and agency stakeholders were already assembled in Oreo's command center, the team was able to quickly design and approve a social media post about the blackout to be pushed out across the brand's channels. The result? The now famous "Dunk in the Dark" tweet—a simple image of a backlit Oreo with the copy "Power Out? No Problem. You can still Dunk in the Dark." With this single piece of content and with $0 in media support, Oreo garnered over 525 million impressions in over 100 countries around the world solely through consumer sharing and press coverage.

Why did it happen?

As Oreo discovered, this contextual model of advertising is powerful, offering consumers highly relevant branded content when they want it the most. When cleverly tied to one of the nation's biggest stages like the Super Bowl, a branded message can reach far beyond traditional viewership demographics by placing that brand at the center of the conversation, both online and offline.

While real-time marketing seems commonplace today—consider Arby's well-deserved success at the 2014 Grammys (correlating the infamous hat worn by Pharrell Williams with their infamous logo) and the slew of arguably dumb Royal Baby posts—the Dunk in the Dark was really the first of its kind, especially given its lack of paid media support.

With this one tweet, the idea of real-time marketing and culture-jacking went from a loosely defined and experimental idea to the premier marketing infatuation of the moment. Shattered were the notions of what made a successful ad during the big game, which went from a $4 million TV spot to a simple image constructed in minutes, shared for free over social media.

Further bulking up the idea of context here is the fact that Oreo was able to execute this content piece in such a timely manner. Perhaps the most important tenet of real-time marketing is the speed with which a brand is able to get their content live. In this case, the blackout proved the perfect setting for Oreo to capitalize on a captivated audience actively seeking information on what was going on in the Superdome via social media; and by being the first brand to comment, they were also the first brand to surprise and delight consumers. Although this lightning in a bottle is difficult to recreate, that hasn't stopped brands from trying to do so. One only need to consider the advent of the "social media war room" that has happened since Dunk in the Dark to see this is true.

Delivery also played an enormous role in the success of Dunk in the Dark. Oreo's team disregarded traditional views on Super Bowl advertising and instead capitalized on trends that were playing a tremendous role in changing viewership patterns. While the Super Bowl is still advertising's biggest stage, the advent of the second screen—the use of a mobile or tablet device to enhance viewing—has greatly changed the way people watch TV.

This phenomenon plays itself out most significantly during television's seminal moments, and in particular, live sporting events, as viewers are increasingly turning to their second screens for enhanced viewing experiences and commentary on social networks. This type of viewing brings events like the Super Bowl and the Oscars to a whole new level. Now it is not just the family gathering around the TV to watch the big game but instead a national and even global audience connected as a community via digital technology.

Oreo took advantage of this phenomenon by choosing social media as their medium of choice, allowing their audience not only to receive their branded content but to interact with it through shares, likes, and retweets. Dunk in the Dark transcended traditional Super Bowl demographic-driven targeting and instead reached consumers in a more relevant and engaging way.

What does this mean?

The Oreo tweet marked a sea of change in advertising from the days of Ed Sullivan because it changed the way marketers think about reaching their key consumers. For the first time ever, the ad that won the Super Bowl—clearly the last great bastion of traditional demographic advertising—did not even run on TV. It was cheaper, faster, and more relevant than any 60- or 30-second spot run during the game could ever be.

The success of Oreo's outreach to the press around the Dunk in the Dark tweet also cannot be downplayed. Perhaps their biggest coup was connecting with Buzzfeed, arguably the biggest drivers of "viral content" in today's online world, minutes after the tweet went live. Other brands like Audi and Tide also recognized the blackout as a perfect opportunity to insert themselves into the Super Bowl conversation online; however, neither brand executed as perfectly as the Oreo team's full court press on the advertising, marketing, and consumer general interest trades. Given their willingness to shop their story around, it is no surprise that they were able to yield mainstream notoriety.

In fact, Dunk in the Dark was so successful that most people forget that Oreo also had a television spot that aired prior to the blackout. With that single tweet, Oreo identified the right moment with the right people and capitalized on the moment with a strong delivery through social media. Brands trying to recreate this type of real-time miracle are frequently lacking on one or both sides of the equation. The need to identify a receptive audience for a brand message in this new science of media—one in which audiences expect their branded content to be timely, relevant, and clever—has led advertisers to embrace the potential of big data.

Psy Oppa and the YouTube Revolution

YouTube, like so many other thriving social networking tools, shot out into popular culture like a cannon. What reality TV shows demonstrated in the nineties is that we crave authentic content from real people. With YouTube, a consumer-generated video tool was introduced that took reality to the next level, anyone could star in their own version of *The Real World* or *The Bachelor*.

After only 10 years of existence, the world was already spending six billion hours a month watching videos on YouTube. More important, 100 million hours of video are being uploaded to YouTube every minute—videos that are created not by "big media" but by people like you and me.

In July of 2012, a little known Korean pop star named Psy Oppa uploaded a quirky music video of a song called *Gangnam Style* and before long created the musical interpretation of Oreo's Dunk "In The Dark" using many of the same principles.

Thanks in large part to a brilliant marketing strategy involving data, context, and delivery, the *Gangnam Style* video has now been viewed over two billion times in a world with a population of seven billion, making it quite possibly the most viewed piece of entertainment content ever created. All of the power of traditional "big media" combined has been unable to create the galvanizing global scale that a former D-list Korean pop star was able to create with an Internet connection and a dream. *Gangnam Style* transcended demographics by its scale alone.

What appears to have happened entirely by chance, however, is actually another carefully choreographed case study in brilliant state-of-the-art Internet marketing. In today's data-driven age, few successful campaigns occur by accident. In this instance, Psy Oppa's team leveraged a powerful and influential delivery approach to create a global phenomenon.

When *Gangnam Style* launched, the video gained immediate credibility in South Korea as the video enjoyed cameos from three local stars: Hwang Min Woo from *Korea's Got Talent 2* No Hung-chul, a popular comedian; and Yoo Jae-suk, a popular TV host. This created a groundswell of interest within Psy's local market.

Gangnam Style's sudden surge in popularity throughout South Korea garnered the interest of Western media, resulting in stories from the likes of Billboard and Gawker. Psy then made the brilliant decision of bringing on American super-manager Scooter Braun, who also represents the greatest musical force born on the Internet: Justin Bieber. Braun's promotion of Psy through his social media channels attracted the interest of tens of millions of "Beliebers," Bieber's social media fan base. Finally, Psy started to capture the interest of American celebrities and *Gangnam Style* became the subject of tweets from Katy Perry and Britney Spears.

The strategic use of influencers in an organic and earned fashion greatly intensified the effects of a catchy song and clever music video to make Internet history. There are scores of lessons to be learned here for all marketers, not the least of which is that you always need the help of others to truly "go viral."

Music Disrupted

As evidenced by *Gangnam Style*, the science of hit making in the entertainment industry has entered a new era. Today, the birth of music platforms like Spotify and Soundcloud forever transformed the way we listen to music the same way that YouTube has disrupted the way we watch content. Despite the fact that iTunes created a first mover advantage in the digital music revolution, it turned out that consumers were craving more infinite choices in music like they had found in video content via YouTube. iTunes is a paid model, but over time it became apparent that consumers wanted to sample music without the commitment of paying, yet another way in which access is trumping ownership in YouthNation.

The 2.0 versions of music platforms are based on "all you can listen" subscriptions, and leverage recommendation engines, based on what friends are listening to, creating a wealth of new music options for consumers. Platforms like Soundcloud allow anyone to upload their own music, not just the privileged artists who can get on iTunes.

The impact of these platforms has been profound on the music industry. In the old era, big media controlled what we heard based on what they thought "the kids were listening to," which forced artists into generic genres and stifled creativity. Now artists have the ability to create new genres and publish their own work, giving anyone the opportunity to produce the next *Gangnam Style*, not just those who caught lightning in a bottle on YouTube.

Viral Can Be Mainstream

With today's wealth of new platforms, the media landscape has evolved from limited forced programming fed to us by big media into an unlimited world of content choices provided by users and independent artists just like us. Now advertising like Oreo's Dunk in the Dark and art like *Gangnam Style* can become smash hits without reliance on big media. Our choices are no longer being determined by big media's preconceived notions of who we should be, or what we should be watching or listening to. Today we are all slowly evolving culture together, and defining our own personal demographic profile with each stream of *Gangnam Style* or bite of an Oreo cookie.

A Conversation with Jonathan Perelman Vice President, BuzzFeed Motion Pictures

Perhaps no other company has redefined the business of digital media in the era of YouthNation more profoundly than BuzzFeed. Founded in 2006 as an experimental lab that focused on tracking viral content and making things people wanted to share, BuzzFeed now serves content to over 175 million people each month. Content of which is curated not by the direction of big media but rather by the audience itself. BuzzFeed's content is nontraditional and cuts across mass demographics. Buzzfeed is the poster child for the future of media. I was compelled therefore, to connect with Jonathan Perelman to get his insights on the disruption he is seeing in this dynamic industry.

Matt Britton: What impact has social media had on traditional broadcast models, and how has BuzzFeed capitalized on that?

Jonathan Perelman: There is no question that social media is the new distribution, and we recognized that at BuzzFeed early on. Whereas the broadcast model focused on centralized TV and print media sources distributing content to the masses, the social web model relies on the power of disparate groups of people—and their individual influence—to distribute content democratically. BuzzFeed knows this, viewing social as the new distribution channel—building its empire against this new way we connect and communicate with each other.

Matt Britton: With people driving distribution, instead of old school media conglomerates, how has BuzzFeed taken advantage of this trend in terms of content creation?

Jonathan Perelman: BuzzFeed focuses on understanding the art and science of sharing—breaking news; writing bold, investigative pieces; and creating entertaining content and videos that are built for sharing among individual groups of people. That can be anything. Unlike the older TV model, "even very specific content can reach a giant audience through the emotional force of sharing." This means creating content not for mass appeal, but rather for the right audience.

Matt Britton: How does BuzzFeed content cut across traditional demographics?

Jonathan Perelman: Our content and news is made for people. We base our content philosophy on three pillars. First, identity. People naturally want to feel like part of a group or "tribe." This type of content capitalizes on this behavior by conveying part of the sharer's identity—so that they'll want to share that truth with their fellow tribesmen. The interesting part is, these tribal "truths" or identities can span across traditional demographics, genders, faiths, races, and age groups. The point is that it brings niche audiences together around a certain passion, and makes them want to share.

Our second pillar is emotional giving. In this type of content, the sharer may have experienced a certain powerful emotion upon viewing the content, and wants to bestow that feeling on their friend. It's a way of saying: "this made me sad/happy/angry—and I think you would feel that way too." Again—traditional demos don't even come into the picture here. What makes us share is the feeling—and we'll share it to whoever we feel will best reciprocate that feeling.

Our third pillar is information. At a most basic level, people want to share information that makes them feel and look smart to their friends, or demonstrates a certain opinion or belief that they may hold.

This means giving them new, unique, or different ways to present information to their peer group

Matt Britton: What is the BuzzFeed bottom line?

Jonathan Perelman: Getting your message heard is only as powerful as getting your message shared. For today's marketers, think about the content you're creating, and ask yourself "Is this something you would share with your friends?" Worry less about mass appeal, and instead tailor your content by honing in on emotions, identities, and information that will drive sharing among powerful, influential niche audiences.

Big Data 101

Any business that wants to reach consumers is now playing a different game. The traditional path of "spray and pray" or blasting out messages to as many as possible has forever lost its potency. This change has created a new way to target consumers, which is more efficient, measurable, and relevant than ever before. With the withering of a mass market on television and the eventual end of mass scale (with few exceptions like the NFL) as a true asset in targeting consumers, a powerful new element has come into play that if used correctly, can make marketing and advertising more impactful than ever: that element is big data.

Big data is a term used to describe the collection of large, complex data sets gathered from consumers by brands and platforms. The information compiled in these sets could range from demographic information, such as income and race, to behavioral information, such as consumer trends, to environmental factors, such as weather and geopolitical impact.

The collection of this data, and its subsequent analysis, helps brands see correlational relationships across markets that transcend the old model of simple mass market demographics. Big data helps concretize what could be relevant for you as an individual consumer. This, in turn, leads to better decision making by brands when targeting a specific audience in an advertising campaign. Simply put, brands can now deliver the right message to the right consumer at the right time far more easily. And not just during Super Bowl blackouts.

The Three Pillars of Big Data Access

The notion of big data when it comes to advertising is really nothing new. For years, advertisers have had the luxury of targeting consumers. With the explosion of social media though, the notion of big data has gotten even bigger, highly sophisticated, and more potent:

1. **Data:** *We have more data than ever before on consumers.* The proliferation of social networks has created powerful data sets of what people like (the interest graph) and whom they know (the social graph) which can be used in ways there were unimaginable before. Mark Zuckerberg revealed in a 2014 internal interview that Facebook has indexed over one trillion posts from users.

2. **Platforms:** *There are powerful venues to target consumers based on this data.* The massive adoption of new consumer platforms created by bellwethers like Facebook and LinkedIn allow us to reach consumers at scale in a data-fueled environment, increasingly on mobile devices.

3. **Products:** *We have new tactics to reach consumers.* Social networks have developed an amazing array of ad products to reach consumers with the right message at the right time which in some cases blur the lines between content and advertising.

The Social and Interest Graph

One of the most important changes that has emerged from the social web and its treasure trove of big data is the ability to create a dynamic and unfiltered view of the content and topics consumers are most interested in engaging with at every moment. Marketers no longer have to rely on generically broad and arguably unreliable measuring sticks for what consumers want to see, which as we all know is a moving target. The social web has opened up an entirely new data set: graph metrics, which if analyzed right, functions almost like individual fingerprints by tracking relationships and interests of individuals and the public at large in real time. For example, if there is an emerging trend, talent, or product, marketers can now see these groundswells bubbling immediately. Brands now have the ability to rapidly respond by delivering content based on where the interest and demand lies.

The power of this data is just now being realized by businesses big and small and is in many ways leveling the playing field in terms of a small brand's access to large-scale consumer audiences. Interest and social graphs are two ways that marketers can use big data to discover the little things that make all the difference.

The interest graph

A hallmark in the evolution of social media tools has been the ability for consumers to "like" what they are looking at on platforms like Facebook or Instagram and broadcast it for the world to see. In many ways the "like" has turned into the shortest and most potent form of consumer content, as it is generated with a single click. By liking something, whether it's a sports highlight, a friend's photo, or a branded Facebook page, a consumer is signaling to friends, the content producer, and the Web at large what matters to them.

The aggregation of likes has allowed the public and brands to get a realistic and highly specific view into what consumers really enjoy and where their interests truly lie: This is the interest graph as illustrated in Figure 13.1. No longer do we need to rely on big media to tell us that the suburban kids were into skateboarding by way of the latest sitcom, or wait for MTV to tell us about a hot new band. Consumers now have the power to dictate trends, create movements, and evolve culture independently of big media. And now brands have a way to measure and leverage this treasure trove of interest information in new, highly specific, personal, and innovative ways that can drive scale in ways never before imagined.

An interest graph also allows brands to make assumptions about other interests a consumer holds based on his/her own selections. In a larger sense, it helps brands understand what they can suggest as relevant to *you*, individually, especially in a digital marketplace

When aggregating user interest data, they become "nodes" in a complex web. Using social network analysis, brands can then identify clusters of similar communities, known as "lookalike audiences," which, when viewed on an aggregate scale, can help inform brands on similar communities' interests, taking guesswork out of the equation. Marketers now have the ability to become laser focused on who is most likely to want to hear from them, and when.

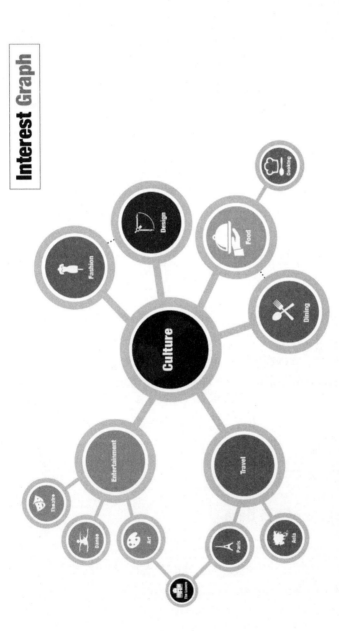

FIGURE 13.1 The interest graph is a powerful data source for real-time consumer behavior (Created by MRY)

179

The social graph

Everyone knows that our friends in social media don't exactly mirror our friendships in real life. There is, however, a good deal of value that marketers can glean from your "social graph."

A social graph as illustrated in Figure 13.2 is a digital map that connects who people are, who they are connected to, and who is likely to influence them online. In short, it represents digital relationships and how they fit into larger, online communities. A practical application of this data would be a user joining a new social network and having his contacts from other networks automatically imported and recommended for him to connect to on the new network.

On a smaller level, once a company "understands" your taste, it can suggest further, relevant options that *feel* tailored to you, but actually arise from the millions of other relationships that exist in "big data" that the brand has already analyzed and considered. This is why when you are on Facebook, movies are suggested for you to check out because your friends like them, or they are otherwise likely to interest you.

The future of big data

As the rampant use of social networks continue, and unimagined quantities of data gets collected on all American consumers and particularly YouthNation, platforms and marketers will gain an unprecedented amount of insight and knowledge on consumer behavior.

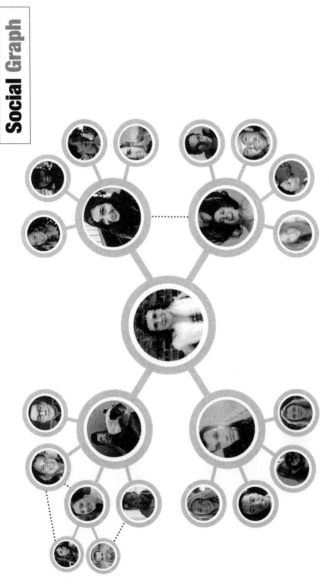

Social Graph

FIGURE 13.2 The social graph is a real-time view into the vast web of human relationships formed across the social web (Created by MRY)

Soon, big data will power and customize every message that is delivered, from the songs that play in your car, to the billboards that you see when you cruise the highway, to the coupons that appear on your phone at the market, to the commercials you view when you get home (on a television screen that is really a computer). The data will likely become so robust and powerful that marketers will graduate from being addressable or personalized to predictive, or providing consumers with product and service recommendations before consumers have even asked for them. We will truly enter the Jetson age.

Big data stands to create enormous value for companies like Facebook (which also owns Instagram) who will continually find new ways to monetize its data, selling information to any business trying to influence a prospective buyer. For YouthNation this will likely come with an expectation that messages will only be served which are relevant and contextual. Marketers of all sizes will need to tap the scientific side of advertising to have a shot at being heard by the next generation of consumers. Big data is indeed here to stay.

CHAPTER 14

People Are Brands

Youth culture has always created its own brand of alternative celebrities, influencers and counterculture gurus who expressed a worldview that mirrored the thoughts and concerns of the young, in an adult-driven world that rarely reflected their actual beliefs. In the past, these counterculture celebrities, who had no access to the mass scale that traditional media could provide, were forced to bang the drum slowly, building from the grassroots of America, and making their presence felt through the force of their point of view, often one person at a time.

They gave poetry readings in back rooms of smoky bars, wrote provocative articles in hand-published and hand-distributed newsletters, staged happenings, delivered radical lectures in university classrooms, and built their brands slowly through word of mouth. While iconic gurus and influencers like Timothy Leary, Noam Chomsky, Abbie Hoffman, or Angela Davis did ultimately amass a following and influence culture, their audience and their access remained niche.

Flash forward to today's world where social media has created a platform to access audiences on a mass scale, available to anyone with a point of view to share. Suddenly, YouthNation's counterculture niche influencers of yesteryear are becoming the mainstream celebrities and mass scale influencers of our world, sometimes for better, sometimes for worse.

The Newsfeed Is the New Soapbox

Thanks to the proliferation of 4G data plans, push notifications, and our deep-rooted need for connection, the newsfeeds on popular social media networks, like Twitter, YouTube, Facebook, and Instagram, are a critical part of each day for YouthNation on a 24-hour cycle. These scrolling feeds have become, in many ways, the central source for news, entertainment, information, and commercialism in our lives.

Perhaps the most engaging element of the newsfeeds that drive obsessive mindshare and consumption is the melting pot of informational sources it presents. We're swiping through our friends' baby photos in between brand advertisements and breaking news. Mashed right next to one another is an endless stream of content from your neighbor, the local Pizza shop, CNN, and Beyonce. Never before have individuals and organizations of all sizes experienced a level playing field within the same medium.

Whether we are a business, individual, nonprofit, or politician, we're in a constant battle for the attention and mindshare of our audience. And now, for better or worse, we're competing for the same real estate. That means your ability to have friends see your honeymoon photo album is based on how well your images stack up against Nike's post featuring the new Lebron James sneakers. And the same goes for Nike who is competing against you and me for the attention of their consumer target. Social media no longer distinguishes between the individuals that matter to you and the brands you patronize. Increasingly, people are most certainly brands.

The Democratization of Celebrity

As we've explored, the linear path of getting a degree and working hard to achieve success just isn't enough anymore. In a world of blended newsfeeds, the ability to break through is largely dependent on one's ability to achieve a certain level of fame and visibility, through the news you are sharing about yourself to your world.

For young professionals trying to break through and gain a scholarship, nail that killer internship, or kick-start their career, the stakes for achieving a successful digital personal brand presence are massive. One must find a way to stand out among a sea of competitors to reach the decision makers that matter.

The truth is we all shop like mom does at Wal-Mart: We buy the brands we know. Just like we will always trust throwing Tide or Diet Coke into the shopping cart, we will always trust hiring someone we have heard of: a familiar name or face that feels safe, trustworthy, and like a "known entity."

Years ago I had an indelible experience working with a marketer at a major software company. As an early adopter of social media, he was the first to write a blog and always raised his hand to speak at industry conferences. He was active on Twitter and shared everything he was doing. Over the years, despite what I perceived to be a notable lack of skills when compared with his peer set, he would rise through the ranks as management continued to bank on his notoriety versus his aptitude for the job. It was clear that a new set of criteria were in place for evaluating employee performance, and an individual's Q rating was now a big part of the package.

This is happening everywhere. Fame has been democratized and those who have learned to harness it have put their career on steroids. Imagine doing this *and* being talented—you'd be unstoppable!

While this comes naturally to some, the art of building one's persona can seem elusive and even a bit unorthodox to others. The path to building a personal brand, however, is not really that mysterious, and very similar to building a corporate brand. There is a science to it that can be easily mastered with a little practice.

YouthNation tips for building a personal brand

Following these simple steps could make all the difference in fast-tracking your next promotion or landing your next mega-deal in your personal success story.

1. **Create a consistent personal social media brand.** This means that if possible, try to get the same screen-name or handle on all of the major platforms. If you are named Jane Smith, securing your actual name is all but impossible at this stage in the game so you may need to be creative. Play around with common industry terms or even your college alma mater to create something distinct and ownable. (i.e., Jane Smith could become "BuckeyeJane" if she went to Ohio State).

2. **Activate your presence across as many popular social media platforms as you can to manage**. First start with the Big 5 (Instagram, Facebook, Twitter, LinkedIn, You Tube) and if

you're feeling super charged, play around with some secondary platforms (Pinterest, Tumblr, Snapchat). Even if you don't intend to use a platform, lock down your preferred username on top platforms anyway.

3. **Create a singular value proposition.** Ask yourself, "What can I bring my audience every day that they will derive value from?" Maybe you have great recipes, maybe you have a knack for home design, or are astute at tracking industry trends. Whatever that offering is, focus on it and get better at it.

4. **Map out a content strategy and stick to it.** Once you have nailed your value proposition, challenge yourself to a content calendar where you are consistently creating text, audio (podcasts), video, or photo assets to deliver this value. Every now and then, share relevant articles or posts from others in the space. Make this an indispensable part of your job as now it *is* one.

5. **Sprinkle in content about yourself to humanize and let your persona shine.** Nobody wants to be friends with a robot. We're all people—and we appreciate seeing that side in those we do business with.

Keep in mind that you may very well want to create this professional presence separate from your personal presence in social media. People that follow you for your cooking tips probably don't care about your winter vacation photos. Generally, creating a separate social media profile for business purposes can be a smart strategy. Further, you can use different channels for different purposes. Your Twitter profile may be more business-oriented while your Facebook may be more personal. Utilize "friend" lists that allow for selective sharing and make sure to always think twice before posting anything.

The Rise of the Influencer

Today anyone with an iPhone, a bit of talent (or even an extreme lack thereof), and a burning desire to become relevant has the ability to create a valuable personal brand by amassing a meaningful following and becoming an influencer. Those that are successful can achieve a level of fame, wealth, and significance once reserved only for stars in Hollywood. Through the ubiquity of social media, fame and influence can now be quantified and qualified by the publicly accessible data of fans, followers, and engagement rates across social networks.

Influencers have emerged as a driving cultural force in YouthNation. It is individuals, rather than brands, that are commanding the largest voice on social networks and increasingly capturing our time and attention. In fact 9 of the 10 most followed users on Twitter are people, not brands. Mark Cuban, the owner of the Dallas Mavericks, has more Twitter followers than the team itself. David

Berkowitz, the CMO of MRY, has more followers than his employer. Social media has always been about people; therefore, its people not brands that wield the most influence—and power—in modern media.

Twitter totals that tell the story

It's the people, more than the brand, that appeals to followers and friends.

Mark Cuban (@mcuban): 2.7M

    Dallas Mavericks (@dallasmavs): 609K

Erin Andrews (@erinandrews): 2.5M

    Fox Sports (@FoxSports): 1.1M

    Dancing with the Stars (DancingABC): 611K

David Berkowitz: (@DBerkowitz): 27.2K

    MRY (@MRY): 15.9K

Bill Gates (@BillGates): 20.2M

    Microsoft: (@Microsoft): 6.2M

Twitterlebrities

Here are the 10 most followed users on Twitter, 9 out of the 10 are people, not companies:

1. Katy Perry (@KatyPerry) 66M
2. Justin Bieber (@JustinBieber) 61M
3. Barack Obama (@BarackObama) 55M

4. Taylor Swift (@TaylorSwift13) 53M
5. YouTube (@YouTube) 49M
6. Lady Gaga (@LadyGaga) 45M
7. Britney Spears (@BritneySpears) 41M
8. Justin Timberlake (@JTimberlake) 41M
9. Rihanna (@Rihanna) 41M
10. Ellen Degeneres (@TheEllenShow) 40M

Celebrity Endorsement Reimagined

Since the early days of advertising, companies have paid high-profile celebrities to represent their brands and products. This age-old practice is still around today, just in a reimagined form. Social media has democratized "influencer marketing" by making anyone with an average following, a passion, a hobby, or a point of view, as appealing to brand marketers as celebrities once were. Why? Because not only are they significantly easier to identify and engage at scale, but they also offer a level of peer-to-peer authenticity a paid celebrity could never represent.

Core to this practice is the concept that everyone is influential to *someone* about *something*. Whether you're an Internet chef impacting thousands of foodies or a basement gamer fighting dragons alongside three friends, your endorsement is valuable—and smart marketers know that. Understanding how to identify, engage, and activate influencer advocacy is a fundamental imperative for breakout growth and competitive advantage in the new media marketplace.

Here is a guide to the archetypal Internet influencers available to brands today.

The Cyber Celebrity

Celebrity Internet influencers are this generation's reality-TV star, just without the TV and network agenda. In fact, there are now thousands of individuals that have created full-time careers hosting their own shows on YouTube. These shows rarely have agents, sets, scripts or budgets like shows on television. They don't run at a particular time and don't need to be picked up by a network to be seen. In fact, it is the lack of the traditional barriers that make this content so very real and compelling to the millions of subscribers that are logging in religiously.

Digital celebrities understand the influence they yield and use it wisely. Their endorsement, even their time, is in high demand, so don't expect an easy sell if you reach out to them for an endorsement. At this point in their careers, they get approached frequently to hock all varieties of products or feature different brands when communicating to their audiences. The truth is, if there isn't some type of compensation or fair value exchange offered at jump, they may not even respond to your e-mail, tweet, or call. In fact increasingly cyber celebrities are being represented by Hollywood agents like Williams Morris.

At the same time, if leveraged correctly, the celebrity influencer can be the most effective launch pad or campaign accelerator your weekly growth charts have ever seen. If it fits with their personal brand, would be interesting to their audience, and most important, has something in it for them, you may find your new secret weapon right there on YouTube. All it takes is a bit of searching and a compelling offer.

Cyber Celebrity Spotlight: Michelle Phan.   Named   as one of *Ad Age's* 2014 Media Mavens, Michelle Phan was a struggling college student when she posted her first YouTube video, a seven-minute tutorial on "natural makeup" in 2007. In just a week, it had over 40,000 views. By 2009, she was approached by YouTube to join their partner program. Soon, brands were knocking at her door, including L'Oreal, which gave Phan her own makeup line.

Phan now boasts well over seven million loyal subscribers and has starred in a Dr. Pepper commercial, signed her own book deal, and even appeared in YouTube's latest ad campaign celebrating the network's biggest stars and content creators in an effort to appeal to marketers looking to tap into the power of online video.

The Social Influencer

The social influencer is typically someone with a special interest in one or more related topics and enjoys creating content to share with friends and fellow community members, likely through their blog. Their knack for creativity and interesting perspective help build up a nice following, and they find themselves wielding an audience of several thousand like-minded individuals, eager to hear from and share with them.

The social influencer is easier to engage than the cyber celebrity, because they don't get the same volume of inbound requests and have significantly less reach. While at the same time, there's an argument that the social influencer's endorsement is more impactful proportionately (per follower) because they tend to have stronger, more trusted relationship with their following.

The key to engaging social influencers is to deliver true value. Don't give them prepackaged tweets to share on your behalf; they're smarter than that. Give them the products to try for themselves, and even samples to give away across their social channels. If you try and under-value their advocacy, they'll see right through it. In fact, you even risk them posting negatively about you if your outreach offends them, for any reason whatsoever.

Social influencers want to feel "in the know." Tip them off on product launches and other important intel before it hits the press. Invite them to an "influencer" event or some other exclusive opportunity. It's helpful to seed information through them, so it hits the public through word-of-mouth chatter, rather than through mainstream media.

Influencers will take every opportunity to reinforce their importance and be socially validated. Partnering with Internet influencers increases a brand's authority in any particular space. Don't underestimate the power that aligning with your brand gives them, but don't treat them as corporate sell-outs either. Truth and authenticity are at the core of everything they do; make sure to remember and empower that.

Social influence spotlight: Blogher

As young millennial women who grew up with the Internet in the household started to have children, a new class of social influencers emerged. Stay-at-home moms armed with an inherent knowledge of social media formed the mommy blogger community. Smart, educated, passionate women need an outlet to voice their opinions, and blogging and social media has proved to be a critical channel for them.

The power of the mommy blogger is rooted in the fact that moms are indeed the CEOs of the American household. When it comes to shopping for their family, especially their children, mom has become increasingly skeptical of commercial messages. Who does she trust? Other moms. As mommy bloggers amassed followings and influence, corporate marketers selling everything from Huggies to Hondas clamored to inform what mom bloggers wrote and what new products they covered and endorsed.

Today the mommy blogger community is a force of nature on the Internet. They have proven their ability to create blockbuster products and tear others down. The influence of the mom bloggers has even spurred the launch of companies like Blogher (now SheKnows), predominantly a network of mom bloggers and a great way for brands to leverage this critical audience. Blogher has transformed into a cross-platform media company that boasts a reach of over 100 million women each month through their community of social media and blog influencers.[1]

For brands, the Blogher network of over 3,000 quality bloggers and 12,500 social media personalities offers a unique opportunity to engage with female consumers in an authentic and persuasive dialogue. Custom branded content created by network members also has the opportunity to not only reach the audience of the creator but to also be amplified by Blogher across platforms, transforming digital advertising into word-of-mouth. With bloggers and influencers also paid for their contributions to campaigns that run on their personal networks, it's a win-win-win for Blogher, the content creator, and the brand in play.

Given the purchasing power that women hold, it is no surprise that brands in even the most unexpected categories look to tap into Blogher's audience. For example, Bridgestone Tires acted as a sponsor of the Blogher 2014 conference, even hosting a "No Pressure Zone" that offered mimosas and massages for conference attendees.

The Everyday Influencer

The everyday influencer is your typical consumer, going about their daily lives. They have average social network size and sphere of influence, but they are passionate ambassadors of the brands they embrace, and feel *great* about telling their friends. The question is, how do you ensure that *you* are being talked about, not your competition. The stakes for achieving everyday influence is now front and center for all brands.

At MRY, we tackle this challenge for clients by designing social behaviors into every touch point of the consumer journey, which creates sharing and advocacy from awareness through conversion. From the moment they see an ad for your product to the point of consumption, we ask ourselves how can we integrate advocacy into the user experience. If we strategically lower the barriers for sharing, how many more people will tell their friends? Everyone is always looking for a good story to tell. It's incumbent upon brand marketers to ensure that they're part of the story.

Make your everyday influencer feel special by giving them a voice, and investing in theirs. Surprise and delight them with tokens of your appreciation for their loyalty. Reward their participation and advocacy with brand love, in the form of merchandise, discounts, product, and additional pass alongs for their friends. The occasional exclusive opportunity will go a long way.

Every customer you have is an everyday influencer. How well you unlock their full potential is determined by your understanding of what motivates them to share, and what they love about your brand. Embed "talkable" touch points into the core of your customer experience and word-of-mouth will quickly become your strongest marketing asset.

Everyday Influencer Spotlight: Old Navy Style Council

Old Navy approached MRY and its partner word-of-mouth software platform CrowdTap (now a separate company) in the hopes of tapping into the everyday influencers that were already advocating for their brand online as well as recruiting new ones. As a result the Old Navy Style Council was created as an online forum for the brand's biggest fans.

The Style Council was used to encourage key influencers to evangelize the brand on their own social channels by promoting new and exclusive content, offers, and events. CrowdTap's platform also allowed Old Navy to gauge consumer insights by having these same advocates participate in polls and discussions and test new lines of merchandise, letting these influencers actually play a role in influencing the brand's decisions around new products. Style council members were also invited to special in-store events and offered party-hosting kits around new product lines, further reinforcing their "insider" status.

With over 63,000 members, the Style Council increased Old Navy's net promoter score by 113 percent and resulted in 1.2 million views of Old Navy online content.

Lessons from the MRY Archive: CrowdTap

In 2010, MRY created CrowdTap, a software platform that allows every consumer to leverage the power of their online influence and impact on the brands they love. The CrowdTap model is illustrated in Figure 14.1. Members of CrowdTap that are selected by participating brands have the ability to get rewarded through distributing samples, responding to polls, and sharing online content to their on and offline peers. The platform

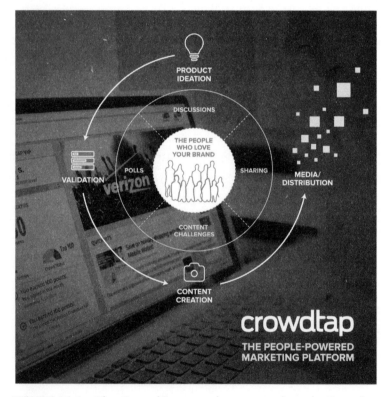

FIGURE 14.1   The CrowdTap people-powered marketing platform (Provided by Crowdtap)

creates a simple and rewarding way for consumers to advocate for the products and services they care about.

Though not often large in size, the followers of everyday influencers are likely personal connections, thus making their advocacy the most powerful on a 1:1 basis through heightened relevancy and trust. The exponential growth in the power of influencers has turned CrowdTap, once a side project, into a booming ad-tech company recently ranked by *Inc.* magazine as the #4 fastest growing company in New York City.

Influence Gone Mainstream

If you don't have a budget to engage a YouTube star, partner with the Blogher network, or activate a platform like CrowdTap you can still leverage the power of influencers to drive your business. That is, of course, if you've managed to create a product or service that is compelling enough that consumers will advocate for it naturally. However, even with a great offering, your ability to generate advocacy is not guaranteed. These are real people after all. You need to offer a compelling value exchange to foster customer advocacy and brand love.

As the power of homegrown individual influencers continues to explode, their presence is now bubbling up to the surface of traditional media. The scale of influence that the Michelle Phan's of the world have has now crept into the world of traditional television. No longer are the networks and studios deciding who enters your home; it is the stars the people have chosen who are now gaining this exposure.

Unlike in the past, when TV content influenced digital content, today the roles have reversed and digital media and the influential luminaries it has created are now playing a transformative role on stodgy old television as broadcast bigwigs and big brands look to the popularity of online stars to become the next television and movie stars.

Online stars who become TV stars

Here are some notable examples of how digital video is shaping TV, as the YouTube stars of yesterday become the TV stars of today.

Billy on the Street. It's hard to imagine that Billy Eichner ever imagined being called "comedy's next big thing" when he posted his first YouTube video nearly a decade ago. Eichner has made a career out of his obnoxious yet hilariously funny man-on-the-street style interviews, where he has zero concern about harassing New Yorkers with questions like, "For a dollar, do you think Prince puts down the moon as an emergency contact?"

TV networks took notice as his videos started amassing millions of views and followers online, and in 2011 Eichner was approached by Fuse TV with an offer to do his own series in conjunction with Emmy-winning comedy video website Funny or Die. *Funny or Die's Billy on the Street* just ended its third season and has featured cameo appearances from celebrity fans like Will Ferrell, Drew Barrymore, and Amy Poehler.

Maker's Studio and Disney.   In March of 2014, Disney
purchased YouTube's Maker Studios in a deal worth up to
$950 million. Maker Studios is one of the largest produc-
ers and distributors of online video content to millennial
audiences, attracting over 6.5 billion views and 450
million monthly subscribers.[1] Disney, which owns more
than a dozen broadcast and cable networks, still hadn't
managed to find much digital success, an increasingly
concerning fact given the rapidly growing numbers of
people that are cutting the traditional TV cord. Maker's
gigantic roster of up-and-coming and established young
online talent gave Disney an immediate boost.

Now, it looks like Disney is planning to use this
partnership to not only improve their online presence
but their more traditional networks as well by high-
lighting that same talent on TV. Disney and Maker
just announced their plans to produce holiday TV
specials featuring digital talent for the Disney Channel
and Disney XD. Maker is also reportedly working on
TV-first content for Disney Channels worldwide. Given
how many of today's popular young celebrities have
risen through the ranks of the Disney Channel to find
mainstream stardom, we can assume that many of Maker's
faces will soon become just as familiar.

Grumpy Cat's Worst Christmas Ever.   Even if you call
yourself a dog person, there is no denying that cats
hold a powerful place in the hierarchy of the World
Wide Web. The entertainment industry has taken notice
and is hoping their meme-able magic will rub off on
traditional media. In fact, the Internet's most popular

ornery feline, Grumpy Cat, recently signed a movie deal with Broken Road Productions. The first film in this deal, *Grumpy Cat's Worst Christmas Ever*, debuted on Lifetime during the 2014 Christmas season and featured *Parks and Recreation* star Aubrey Plaza as the voice of the titular cat.

The influence of Internet cats has expanded to the big screen, too. In 2013, Vice premiered their full-length feature film, *Lil Bub & Friendz*, at the Tribeca Film Festival. The film explored the popularity of Bub and his "cat-lebrity" counterparts and won the Best Feature Film award at the festival.

Drunk History. Who doesn't love their history with a shot (or entire bottle) of whiskey? *Drunk History* began as a Web series in 2007 in which a narrator—typically a comedian or actor—gets extremely wasted on camera and proceeds to tell a story from America's history, from how Benjamin Franklin discovered electricity and Abraham Lincoln's assassination to lighter fare like the creation of the hip-hop hit "Rapper's Delight." As the narrator stumbles through the drunken interpretation of famous historical narratives, actors perform the scenes from the often hilarious, unpredictable drunken utterances of the narrator. This may sound silly, and it is, but it is also incredibly funny and surprisingly informative.

After featuring stars like Jack Black and Ryan Gosling, the Web series attracted a cult following. Comedy Central picked up the show in 2012, and it was recently renewed for its third season, making it perhaps the only show on TV that requires an onsite medic during filming to ensure that its participants don't get too drunk.

A Conversation with Danielle Tiedt, CMO, VP Marketing, YouTube

Danielle Tiedt, someone whom I've worked with for nearly a decade, dating back to her stint at Microsoft's Bing, is the CMO, VP of Marketing at YouTube. In her role, Danielle is at the center of the "People Are Brands" revolution helping to shepherd in a new era of content consumption and entertainment for YouthNation at one of the world's leading online platforms. I spoke with Danielle about what she is seeing unfold in this exciting space.

Matt Britton: Say I'm someone who really wants to be the next Michelle Phan. What advice do you have for people looking to build their personal brand through YouTube?

Danielle Tiedt: The first piece of advice is to be really true and authentic to you. We see over and over that people relate to people on YouTube who are true to themselves and authentic in their story. It's almost like they found a friend, and then they become passionate fans because they feel like they're having this conversation with this person who has a story that they can relate to.

The second piece of advice is to be brave, take chances, and commit. Like anything in life, really, you aren't going to just be famous or put a video up and all of a sudden become a face that everyone recognizes. It takes commitment and hard work and consistency.

Matt Britton: In terms of the success stories on YouTube, how much of that success can be attributed to the quality of the content and how much can be attributed to a good understanding of the mechanics of distribution?

Danielle Tiedt: Hank Green just came out with a great thought on what it takes to make content successful on YouTube. He was one of the first real creators on YouTube, and he has this really thoughtful conversation about what it takes to be successful on YouTube today, and I completely agree with him. He said that one of the biggest things that you need to understand is that your content just needs to be a little bit better than everything else on YouTube. That is the stuff that ends up becoming really successful. What this means is that your content needs to be good enough that people really relate to it, but it has that little bit of special sauce in that everyone who views it thinks, "I could have done that too."

So the rule of the medium is that the stuff that works really, really well is the stuff that is just a little bit better than everything else on YouTube. So if you think about what it takes to build that, it becomes really simple. It relates back to being true and authentic to yourself and working hard to figure out how you're going to tell that story to an audience and then being brave, taking chances, and committing.

It doesn't take big production budgets to make something happen on YouTube. The great thing about YouTube is that from day one you have the ability to reach a billion people immediately all across the world and find your fan base, but you have to be really regular with your uploads. That's what our algorithm catches on to. It helps the people who are doing regular uploads because they are getting more people to watch more videos and that's what gets you ranked higher, which gets you more eyeballs, which gets the whole flywheel working.

Matt Britton: As more and more people start to use mobile devices to consume content, do you see that short-form content is working better than long-form content?

Danielle Tiedt: Our average watch time right now is 30 minutes, so the definition of short form and long form is a little outdated. Is 30 minutes short form or long form? Is long form two hours? Is long form 10 minutes? Those definitions are a little old school and don't map to the reality of what YouTube is today.

Matt Britton: How do you see this groundswell of attention toward YouTube, particularly with the millennial audience, colliding with traditional broadcast television?

Danielle Tiedt: I think that it's something that is really fast evolving because TV is fast evolving. Not to get too meta with it, but you have to ask the question what is TV? Is streaming HBO from your computer TV? I think increasingly it is just going to become content that you watch and where you get it from will become moot.

Brands follow consumer's behavior, so for brands it's the same medium it always was. It just requires new capabilities and understanding. As a brand, you are always trying to understand what your target market is watching and how you can become super authentic in that space. Young Gen C people are on YouTube, so for brands it is just, "How do I show up there in an authentic way?"

It is a question of content versus advertising, and it's about being part of the conversation; it's not just eyeballs. It's about being part of an interactive dialogue and experience with the consumer, which is what we have been talking about in marketing for forever. For the last five to seven years, we have been talking about engagements where they really matter. I think that brands are finally getting what that means as it relates to YouTube. The mistake is when people think of advertising on YouTube the way that you advertise on TV. YouTube is a social channel.

Matt Britton: Which brands are really getting it on YouTube?

Danielle Tiedt: I think Dove Sketches was brilliant. They did a fabulous job of really understanding our platform. The most successful ad ever on YouTube was Turkish Airlines' "Kobe vs. Messi Selfie Shootout," which was built entirely for YouTube. Pepsi has done a great job of really understanding the essence of YouTube. Wal-Mart has been doing a really interesting job working much more on the UGC side. I love when brands get down and dirty with UGC. They're doing a lot of that around the holidays and I love that.

Matt Britton: What are some of the ad products that you see really working well for brands on YouTube?

Danielle Tiedt: Our bread and butter is TrueView where people are choosing to view ads. That is certainly the biggest part of our business—it's an engagement model because when people choose to engage with your ad they remember it more. We just rolled out an app install product that I'm incredibly excited about. It uses TrueView with a click to download for app install, which for Gen C is a big win.

Matt Britton: Do you think YouTube is a driver of fame? Has it helped democratize fame and put it within reach?

Danielle Tiedt: I do. It's been fascinating. YouTube has created a different path to fame. I don't know if you saw the *Variety* article that gave the power index ranking for different stars with the teen audience and basically the top stars for the teen audience are all YouTube stars. I think our generation looks at is as a democratization of star power, but I think teenagers look at it as, "What is a star? I'm looking for people that I relate to." They don't even relate to fame in that way.

Teenagers look for different things in the people that they relate to. It used to be, for us, that we related to big huge movie stars, and it's not that we don't relate to them anymore; they're just looking at a different bar for which they are letting into their life in big ways.

Matt Britton: Some of the big movie stars aren't authentic and relatable in a YouTube world, and then you look at someone like Taylor Swift who is, who has star power *and* gets it and that's why she's able to do what she's doing.

Danielle Tiedt: 100 percent. She is such a good example of that. Too often our generation and advertisers say, "I just don't understand this YouTube star thing" because they're trying to put it in the old context. The stars used to be the water cooler moment, the thing that brought culture together and that we could all come together on. Now, teenagers are much more about their personal relationship with that person.

15

Brands Are People

As we have established, most people use social media to follow people and not brands, so if you want to make your brand shareable and attract advocates you need to turn your brand into a living, breathing persona. In a world where the newsfeed squeezes us all together, now more than ever before, just as people have become brands, brands must become people.

Creating a Brand Persona

Transforming a brand into a living, breathing element is a new challenge for modern day marketers. Traditional advertisers have relied on a brand to speak through its logo and advertising. Today, however, consumers expect to hear from the brand directly. When a brand talks to consumers, it needs to sound authentic, interesting, and engaging. Enter the creation of the brand persona.

Building your brand persona beyond just a logo and a corporate entity will dramatically increase your business's ability to enter the conversation where it counts. It is the only sustainable way to penetrate the newsfeed, where your consumers are undoubtedly spending their time this very moment—both as I type and as you read this. The steps to designing a social brand persona involve three core elements: look, tone, and feel.

The three core elements of brand persona

- **Look:** If you are running a business or a marketing department, then you likely have a logo that adorns your business card or signage. Well now its time to bring the logo to life. The look of your brand persona needs to extend across the fonts you use, the filters you put on images, and even what people are wearing in the photos you post. Do you want your look to be Edgy? Professional? Provocative? Think hard about your brand's new wardrobe and dress for success.

- **Tone:** If your brand were a person, what would it be like? Is it irreverent and spontaneous? Strong and reliable? Brave and adventurous? The first step in the personification of your brand is to establish an identity for it that's intrinsically tied to your business. If you are a banker, be reliable and honest; if you are a baker, be whimsical and decadent. The identity of your brand should reflect your corporate values and the type of employee you want to work for you. Take time to think through word choice and sentence structure, both online and in-store.

- **Feel:** The feel of your brand is reflected in the emotion you are looking to evoke and inspire from every consumer that interacts with it. If you are in the financial services business, you likely want to make people feel safe. If you are a travel agent, you likely want to make people feel inspired. If you are a restauranteur, you likely want to make them feel hungry. This comes through in the design, layout, and aesthetic of everything you do. Think of the difference in a bold font versus light font versus cursive at a subconscious level. Through carefully mastering the feel you're going for, you'll be able to say and reinforce your brand persona and value without saying anything at all.

Once you've established your look, tone, and feel, you will be in a position to bring your brand to life! Extend your brand personality across every touch point of the consumer journey. From in-store signage and menus to your website and social channels, even to the way you answer the phone, everything should look, sound, and feel consistent. Once that's complete, it's time to enter the conversation.

Content Strategy

As we have discussed, you will be competing on social channels with someone's cute baby photos. So in order to achieve optimum results, you will need to be quite strategic about the cadence and quality of content stories your brand will deliver and what your brand's voice will be.

With this in mind, let's explore how to build a content strategy that streamlines the process, ensures you're always on target, and let's you develop/design in advance.

The who, why, and what of brand content

Who?. Who are the different people or types of people making up your community, who have opted in to hear from your brand? Who actually follow you on social media? This is likely made up of your different customer segments: related-interest practitioners/hobbyists, employees, media, competition, friends, and family. Jot down everyone you think could or would follow you on the far left of a whiteboard or piece of paper.

Why?. Why do they follow you? What are their core interests or need states that inspired them to connect with you in the first place? Each "who" category may or may not have a unique why, but think it through. Customers want to hear about new products or service updates. They also want access to the incredible information you provide on the related topics that interest them the most! Your staff wants to represent and celebrate the output of their collective hard work. Friends and family want to keep up on what their loved ones who work for you or use your products care about. Think through every "why"; it's important and it informs the final piece: What?

What?. Knowing exactly *who* your community is and *why* they connect with you will give you the clues that you need to explore *what* kind of content you can create or share that delivers exactly what your audience is looking for. First think through broad brush stroke top line topics, then explore specific topics you'd cover in a blog post or "how-to." Think through all common content types:

how-to, "featured" employees/fans, behind-the-scenes or "exclusive" access to your business, relevant press and articles in the media and pop culture, etc. This should be the most fun part of the exercise because it enables you and the team you pull together for this exercise to get creative and think (way) outside the box. It's better to throw 30 ideas on the whiteboard and end up with 10 solid topics than to come up with only 8 to begin with. Get them all out there, then prioritize which three to five concepts you'll build out first.

With a content strategy in place, you'll need to develop a "content calendar" to organize all of the ideas into an easy-to-manage system that streamlines the whole process. Essentially, a content calendar allows you to plan out the subject matter and sometimes the literal post across each social media channel you manage weeks or even months in advance.

Start by putting in major dates across the year such as holidays, product releases, new store openings, etc. Then overlay pop-culture events like holidays, the Super Bowl, award shows, TV show season premiers—anything your brand persona would watch, do, or participate in if it were a person like you and me.

With that big picture in place, move to the weekly level. How often you should post is different for every community and channel, but if in the content strategy workshop you decided to put out a relevant blog-post once a week, figure out the best day for that and stick to it. This will help you manage and maximize time and resources. The output? You're now consistently publishing relevant and rich content that delivers on the exact reasons your fans are following you. This is where the magic happens.

Community Management

With a growing community, engaged audience, and increased conversation, it's going to be too much for you to handle *and* run your business at the same time. That's a good thing. Your social channels, like any community, need TLC. Someone needs to make sure (and be accountable for) posts going up on time, in the right tone, and of the quality that ensures advocacy and social sharing. Someone needs to continue to build out your content calendar and refine your content strategy based on real-time analytics provided in the back end of each social platform. Enter: the community manager.

A community manager is the individual or team of individuals that run the day-to-day operations involved in maintaining active, engaged brand channels across all social media platforms. They monitor the social conversations for opportunities to engage; they watch for questions from within the community (or anywhere on the wild wild Web) that they can answer, and most of all, they are the living breathing human beings behind your brand persona. More and more, brands are making their community managers outward-facing roles, where customers know the #CMGR by name, and even face, and converse with them as they would another person, instead of a big company.

The community manager role is vital to any brand that is serious about harnessing the full power of social media, and sadly, is often overlooked by smaller organizations. If you can't hire a full-time community manager, create a task force made up of the millennials within your business, or open it up to a team of inspired interns who report to you or your marketing manager. The more present you are in the social conversation about your company/industry and the more engaged your audience, the better your results will be—guaranteed.

CHAPTER

16

A Story Worth Sharing

As children we all loved to be told stories. As our parents flipped through oversized books with images that seemed larger than life, we learned how to understand concepts that connected in a progression to create something lasting. Stories sparked our imaginations and calmly fueled our dreams before sleep. The power of stories has always been magical. It's how we learned early on to connect, share, and explore the world around us. For centuries, it's how we passed forward our histories and culture to future generations. And today, enabled by technology and social media, stories are more present in our daily lives than ever before.

Today, we are bombarded by hundreds, even thousands, of messages from our "friends" and those we follow on a 24-hour cycle. It's the stories we see and hear (rather than the ads we avoid) that make us laugh, cry, or smile: stories that in some ways remind us of our comfy bedtime routines as children.

It's clear that YouthNation is gravitating toward perpetual stories as a primary path in communicating with one another. The ways in which America's youth converse have become never-ending threads of short-form text and image-based messaging which over time tell the story of evolving relationships.

The Death of the Phone Call

The traditional paths by which previous generations communicated with one another when not face-to-face has lost most of its relevance with YouthNation. The reasons why phone calls are going the way of the dodo tell us a lot about the power of storytelling:

- On a telephone call, you can only carry on one conversation at a time. YouthNation is building multitudes of stories with dozens of people, all at the same time.
- The telephone is limited in how you can express yourself. Images, emojis, and animated GIF files provide YouthNation with an abundance of ways to express their feelings while showcasing their creativity.
- The phone is often a disconnected tool. In other words, you aren't assured that someone will pick up on the other end and YouthNation doesn't have time for that. Remember voicemail? Before you know it, that will be a distant memory.

Ironically, even though YouthNation is glued to their smartphones, it isn't to make phone calls. Through perpetual threads of posts, tweets, and Snapchats, multi-level stories are built that are engaging, immersive, and ongoing. Stories, rather than conversations, are now the lifeblood of how YouthNation communicates about or with anything or anyone that matters to them.

Stories versus Conversations

Stories have the ability to become much more powerful than conversation because they have the ability to bring in others over time and take multiple forms that are far more expressive than words. Unlike phone calls, stories never hang up and there is never a busy signal, and someone is always on the other end of the line. In YouthNation stories are truly multimedia allowing for endless expression, uniqueness, and creativity—in real time.

Multimedia storytelling tools

Here are just some of the enhancement tools that turn a conversation into a story worth sharing.

Emojis: as pictured in Figure 16.1, are fast becoming a primary language in the U.S. Instead of actually typing out words, emojis convey emotions and creativity in ways that talking never could, and in shorthand because an image is worth a thousand words. Just like the hieroglyphics used by prehistoric cavemen, emojis are now creating secret languages between groups of peers that evolve overtime. They are becoming a foundational pillar for the exchange of stories.

Tagging: As the popularity of platforms like Instagram continue to expand, "tagging" has also grown

FIGURE 16.1 Emojis are all the rage in YouthNation (Licensed from Shutterstock)

in popularity as a way to communicate by connecting friends to other people's stories. For example, if someone you follow posts a picture of a Calvin Harris DJ show and you share this as a common interest with someone, you will "tag" or add their username to the comment thread on that post and start a conversation. This creates a forum to occur on someone else's post that can start to include everyone that knows the person who is tagged.

Profiles and Avatars: Whether it's a unique username on Snapchat, an ever-changing avatar on Twitter, or a constantly changing bio on Instagram, profiles and avatars are being used to communicate a current state of being and are a core component to creating a shareable story. It's how YouthNation signals the stories they are looking to hear and tell.

Communication Disrupted

As new forms of communication like emojis and tagging become de facto communication tools for YouthNation, many foundational communications tools, far more modern than the telephone, also are now seemingly at risk.

- **E-mail:** While GenX may have grown up during the Web 1.0 age attached to their Blackberry devices answering e-mails 24/7, e-mail is a largely obsolete tool for YouthNation outside of the workplace. The main reason: e-mail is too slow. As crazy as that may sound to someone who grew up without the presence of the Internet at all, stories happen in an instant and so should the communication platform. Even in the workplace new platforms like Yammer (acquired by Microsoft) are being deployed to allow for faster, richer story-based communications than e-mail could ever offer within larger enterprises.

- **SMS text messaging:** Up until just a few years ago, text messaging was *the* default form of communication among teens but now is starting to see a real drop in relevance with YouthNation. A core driver in the decreasing use of text messages is the pricing strategies of the major wireless carriers whom surprisingly still assess a charge for individual text messages on many of their plans. Many upstarts have taken advantage of this trend by providing cross-platform messaging applications that allow users to exchange messages without having to pay for SMS. The most notable alternative messaging app is called WhatsApp, which exploded with teens overseas and was famously purchased by Facebook in 2014 for a whopping $19 billion.

Ephemeral Storytelling

A key underlying driver in the move away from text messages, e-mails, and even messaging on platforms like Facebook and Twitter is the need for stories to lack permanence. It's important for YouthNation that stories create a continuous string of communications, that won't last forever. Text messages create a record on the phone bill, Facebook messages can last forever on the recipient's profile, and for YouthNation, which has grown suspicious about who may be looking at those stories, this is no longer okay.

Since YouthNation craves the freedom to spontaneously share their stories with one another, freedom from future repercussions has become essential. Youth-Nation has a generalized lack of trust in corporations, facilitated in part by witnessing the 2008 financial collapse, and want full control of the content they create, especially the personal stories they share. As a result, we have entered a new phase in communications. The age of ephemeral storytelling has arrived, and may be here to stay. There is now huge value put on stories that are told, heard, and then vanish in an instant. In 2010 two students at Stanford University created a mobile application called Snapchat that today, for much of YouthNation, has become a foundational form of personal communication. Indeed, Snapchat is now used more than the telephone, e-mail, or text messages by YouthNation.

Currently, Snapchat counts over 100 million active monthly users and is by far the social platform used most by YouthNation with 71 percent being under the age of 25.[1] Many outside YouthNation are unaware of or simply don't get Snapchat. Some even think it's a joke. With its juvenile ghost as a logo, youthful renegade leadership, and a misunderstood reputation as a sexting app, it continues to be written off by mainstream America. Facebook, however, isn't writing it off and reportedly tried to buy Snapchat for over $3 billion in 2014.[2] Snapchat, seeing nothing but growth ahead, turned down Facebook, much like Facebook itself did to Microsoft, Yahoo!, and other suitors during its heavy growth curve nearly a decade ago. In late 2014, Snapchat raised a massive venture capital round with the company being valued at over $10 billion.

It seems for now at least, that Snapchat is here to stay. Snapchat has inspired a host of upstart ephemeral platforms such as CyberDust, funded by famed entrepreneur Marc Cuban. YikYak, launched in 2013, is experiencing explosive growth on college campuses as it allows users to post anonymous messaging visible to those in a 1.5 mile radius. The company was valued at over $350 million just a year after its launch. Even Facebook is getting in on the game now planning and implementing ephemeral aspects to some of its messaging products.

Snapchat essentials

Here is everything you need to know about Snapchat:

- It is a free mobile-only application used to build networks of friends to communicate with. Users may remain anonymous if they choose.
- A Snapchat message consists of a new photo or video taken on a smartphone that can be customized with text, emoji, or hand-edited drawing.
- The sender selects how long they want the message to appear on the recipient's mobile device, as fast as 1 second or as long as 10 seconds.

- Once the Snapchat is viewed by the recipient and the clock runs out, the message is gone. If a recipient attempts to screenshot the image the sender is notified, thus ensuring that nothing gets archived without permission of the sender.
- Users can also use Snapchat to engage in functionality that replicates texting while sharing text, photos, and videos. All of this content immediately disappears after you tap to a new screen on your phone.

In the blink of an eye Snapchats are read and gone, and new stories are created. This is the pace of YouthNation. With tools like Snapchat, YouthNation now has a way to instantly communicate with their networks in multitasking form without worrying about the long-term impact of what they may have shared. It has now become the modern day telephone for YouthNation's story-driven culture.

How Brands Can Tell Stories

Brands who have, for decades, worried only about designing the best logo, TV commercial, and print ad are now coming to recognize that their ability to effectively tell stories has become an integral part of their future success. No easy task in the age of Snapchat. It's now the content that brands share rather than the advertising that they buy that will either drive business results or fall upon deaf ears. Brands need to communicate like YouthNation if they want to reach YouthNation.

The fleeting future of advertising

As we explored earlier, consumers are simply not tuning into live TV anymore like they used to. With the exception of live sports (namely the NFL) and a few select live award shows, they have no reason to do so. Before shows could be recorded with the touch of an app, and before TV content could be accessed in countless places besides a traditional television screen, the consumer had no choice but to consume advertising. After all, for well over a half a century brands have taken advantage of their ability to forcibly bombard the population with advertising—and see results.

Today, brands can no longer rely on communicating to their consumers solely with advertising based messaging. Messaging that is created to convey a unique selling proposition or key benefits like "350 horsepower" or "20 percent more absorbent" are not stories and to most, not worth caring about. The fact is that nearly all products being sold are more than suitable to meet the needs of today's consumer. The Ford Focus has more features than you would ever need to safely get from point A to point B. Its bells and whistles would have been viewed as a technical marvel just ten years ago. All skincare products contain the same basic ingredients. The margin of differentiation in most consumer products are slim to none. However, the benefits in differentiating a brand by telling a better story than the next competitor are limitless.

In many ways the changes in advertising driven from the mass adoption of smartphones over the last three to five years have been much more disruptive than the changes that occurred as a result of the widespread adoption of the Internet itself in the late 1990s and early 2000s. When the Internet was first adopted en masse, brands simply transferred their advertising strategy of juxtaposing commercial messages next to the content the audience wanted to see. If Ford's audience were reading a story on ESPN.com, then it would just run a banner ad right next to ESPN's content. This is really not much different than running a commercial in the middle of SportsCenter.

Today however, YouthNation is glued to their phones. A recent study by Web analytics company SDL revealed that consumers aged 18 to 36 check their phones an average of 43 times per day. That's nearly once every 20 minutes of every waking hour, 365 days a year.[3]

When YouthNation is not playing games on their phones, which they are doing nearly one-third of the time when staring at the small screens, they are likely engaging in social media (namely Facebook, which dominates social network consumption globally on mobile devices). While on platforms like Facebook and other mobile social platforms like Twitter, Instagram, and the aforementioned Snapchat, it is predominantly not advertising that is being consumed and shared. In short, advertising really doesn't work on mobile phones like it did on television or even desktop computing.

In this YouthNation-driven society the consumer is now in the driver's seat of the messages they see.

Brands must now learn how to earn, not buy their way into mindshare. This attention can only be earned by providing some sort of value to the target audience; if the value isn't there, brands will simply become unfollowed, unliked, and, thus, unseen. The notion of providing value is a sea change from traditional brand building and one that is not easily cracked.

What has become clear is that in order to win the attention of consumers, the emphasis of a brand marketer's messaging can no longer focus on the product or service being sold but on how what they are offering makes the consumer feel and the ways in which it enhances their life. Therefore, we are increasingly moving out of the era where advertising is how products are sold and into a world where content is truly paramount.

Content versus advertising

There is a stark contrast between the creation of advertising and content. Essentially content is the inverse of advertising; the model is now flipped inside out.

Advertising is constructed of messages that are built to communicate and persuade one to buy what is being sold. In order to create advertising, creative departments form a brief that usually answers a question like, "What makes my product or service unique and how can we communicate this?"

Content is constructed of messaging that adds value to a consumer's life. In order to create content, creators will respond to the question, "Who is my consumer, what are the unmet needs in their life, and where does my brand fulfill those needs?"

By satisfying the unmet needs of their consumer, a marketer will reap the benefits of getting a consumer to engage with their brand in a more meaningful way. If they are really successful in engaging their consumer they may even be fortunate enough to have their content shared. Brand advocacy, as this is referred to, truly is the Holy Grail of marketing: getting consumers to market on a brand's behalf without even being asked. The complexities of creating effective content for consumers are not lost on brand marketers. As the path to attention can no longer be achieved with solely a large budget, marketers are now tasked with evaluating all facets of their messaging to ensure they can create content worth sharing.

The Sharing Imperative

The name of the game in brand marketing today has become how well you tell your story, and how your story connects with people on an emotional level; this blends their rational purchase behavior with an affinity or action on a subconscious level. Beyond building a business around a likeable idea, and more than using striking imagery on your website to stir emotion, you need to reinforce the power of your story with every piece of content you release. The ultimate goal of brand storytelling? Make your story shareable.

With billions of pieces of social content hitting the Internet around the world every day, platforms like Facebook have developed sophisticated methods of knowing precisely what content across your social and interest graph is predicted to be most interesting and relevant to your audience. The power of these algorithms (Facebook's is called "EdgeRank") control what content is seen and what is sadly dumped into a sea of "social waste." These algorithms are always changing and never fully revealed, but across the social web, one thing remains constant: the more engagement a brand's content receives, the more visibility it receives. The retweet, reblog, and "share" buttons are the modern day marketer's bullseye.

If sharing is the most impactful form of social marketing, as well as the end game for each touch-point of the user journey, it is imperative to understand what motivates people to share. Ultimately, we know that people share content on social media to make a statement about themselves, reinforce their personal brand, and to look the best that they can, through carefully curating their social presence to their friends and family across the world. Your brand—your story—needs to hook the community into sharing, by providing them with ways to show the world what they are and what they care about. This ability of a brand to provide consumers with an additional characteristic to share about themselves is the most important part of being a social brand.

People share stories that are idealistic, impactful, and inspirational; stories that move them to laugh, cry, smile; stories that show the world who and what they identify with. When an organization posts on Facebook or Twitter the only people eligible to see that content organically (or without paid advertising) are existing fans and followers. Thus, the real power lies with a brand's fans and followers who have the ability to share its message, through its content, with their social networks—providing the relevance and authenticity consumers have come to demand.

Designed for the flick

Since the modern Web is experienced more often on-the-go and via our mobile devices than the dying desktop format—and with push notifications that keep us glued to our social media newsfeeds, we are constantly checking our smartphones to see our world's latest and greatest. Right now the lifespan of each story we see is roughly the amount of time it takes to swipe down our phone's screen. For YouthNation, stories live and die in an instant—even if the content continues to live on somewhere in the vast social web.

As more stories are now consumed on the smartphone than anywhere else, stories by brand marketers don't only need to add value to a consumer's life, they need to do so in an instant. Content shared by brands disappear as soon as they are briefly seen by a user casually browsing their newsfeed. In the blink of an eye a consumer will decide whether the story is worth digging deeper into, sharing, or flicking right by. In order to capture the attention in the blink of an eye, stories need to be visually arresting and contextually relevant at that very moment.

Paths to Great Brand Storytelling

In addition to the mandates of being relevant and highly visual, there are strategies a brand must pursue to enable it to become a great storyteller and earn its attention with an increasingly elusive YouthNation. Many of these approaches will force marketers to completely reimagine their thinking and communication framework. For startups, local companies, and agile organizations, though, the playing field has indeed been leveled and it is more possible than ever to stand out among a sea of titans in the marketplace through effective storytelling.

The five mantras of great marketing in the age of storytelling

Almost all of the most successful new organizations in recent memory have one thing in common: an inspiring brand story. This story should not be told through a logo or a product, but rather should be the core DNA of the organization itself. According to Nielsen, 92 percent of consumers reported that they want companies to create advertising that feels like a story. The goal for companies with inspiring brands is to maintain stories that are so inspiring and so moving that it becomes hard not to fall in love with their vision.

Ask yourself how was your company founded? What does it stand for? What makes it different? Why does it even exist? Why should people care? The answers to these questions will quickly uncover if you have an inspiring brand story.

What follows are a few great ones.

Create an inspiring brand story: Pencils of Promise

Pencils of Promise is a fascinating organization founded by Adam Braun, an inspiring entrepreneur I'm lucky enough to call a friend and an advisor of. Pencils of Promise is indeed a story worth sharing. While traveling in India and searching for meaning while working as a consultant, Adam approached a young boy in an impoverished area and asked "If you could have anything in the world what would it be?" The boy's answer was startlingly "a pencil." Not a car, a house, or an iPhone—just a pencil.

The impact of this interaction shook Adam to his core and crystalized a major problem in our world: Many children will never have a chance to prosper because they will never be given their right to be educated; in fact, many cannot even afford a pencil. Adam came home from this trip inspired to do something about it and deposited $25 into a bank account and started a "for purpose" (as opposed to nonprofit) organization called Pencils of Promise.

Today, just five years later, Pencils of Promise is a leading global organization which has recently broken ground on its 265th sustainable school in underprivileged areas around the world like Ghana, Guatemala, and Laos. Now tens of thousands of otherwise hopeless children have the promise of an education, and all because Adam met a young boy whose greatest wish was to have a pencil. This is the stuff that incredibly inspiring and shareable brand stories are made of. Refer to Figure 16.2 to see Pencils of Promise storytelling in motion.

FIGURE 16.2 Pencils of Promise storytelling in motion (Provided by Pencils of Promise)

Go deep: Red Bull

Your ability to tell a consistent story to consumers using mobile and social channels is also predicated on the ability to be known for one thing that consumers crave. Just like the books of our childhood, brand stories need to be predicated on a core premise. Unlike our childhood books, though, great brand stories never end and if you have done your job correctly, you will never put your consumers to sleep.

The energy drink Red Bull has set the bar for focused and consistent brand storytelling in the modern era. Red Bull is known for one thing: being extreme. They inspire consumers to push their limits, which plays perfectly into Red Bull's functional benefits of giving you a caffeine-fueled rush.

Since the dawn of the social media era, Red Bull has been ruthlessly focused on creating entertaining content, which their consumers crave in the world of extreme. Flugtag is a sport that Red Bull created which involves pushing handmade flying machines, manned by helmeted people off of tall piers into the water. Sound crazy? Maybe. Some Flugtag events have drawn over 200,000 people to attend. Red Bull uses footage from Flugtag, created by both the brand and its audience, to fuel story-telling about the event participants, venues, creations, and death-defying flights. Instead of sponsoring the X-Games among a sea of me-too brands, Red Bull created its own sport, which is a story they can own exclusively.

In 2012 Red Bull created the ultimate brand story, which will undoubtedly go down as one of the best branded content campaigns in modern history, Red Bull Stratos. The brand teamed with stuntman Felix Baumgartner to attempt to break the sound barrier by flying to the edge of space—an astounding 24 miles above earth—in a helium balloon. As if that weren't enough, they then proceeded to have Felix jump out of the aircraft in a pressure suit at its highest point and freefall back to earth at a speed that broke the sound barrier and a world record. It does not get more extreme than that.

All aspects of this insane experiment were captured through a RedBull-created NASA-like Mission Control Center to tell the ultimate extreme story. The jump itself was broadcast live over YouTube and watched by over 8 million consumers around the world. This is more then the number of people who watched Barack Obama's inauguration. On top of that, Red Bull achieved over 60 million brand impressions on social media and had over 800,000 pieces of consumer content created to support the effort. This was truly great brand storytelling at it's finest for a brand whose slogan is "Redbull gives you wings."

Be human: Dollar Shave Club

When Mike Dubin and Mark Levine founded the Dollar Shave Club, a subscription service for razors, they knew they had to go up against formidable giants like the Procter & Gamble–owned Gillette. They obviously knew they could never compete with the sheer scale that Gillette could provide. Nor could they afford celebrity endorsers like Russell Wilson or Roger Federer. What they did have, however, was an authentic story and the freedom to tell it in an authentic way.

In 2012 right after the company launched, they created and shared a tongue-in-cheek and incredibly clever YouTube video starring Dubin titled *Our Blades Are F*cking Great* (refer to Figure 16.3). The video, which indirectly poked fun at competitors was a smashing success. It told the story of a young renegade with a new company taking on an industry titan. To date, the launch video has been viewed over 17 million times without

FIGURE 16.3 Dollar Shave Club's YouTube breakthorugh (Provided by Dollar Shave Club)

the support of any traditional advertising. Even more incredible is that the video itself drove over \$120,000 in sales in just two days.

Inspire action: Visa

In 2013 MRY client Visa created a storytelling campaign called "Go in Six." The premise of the campaign was simple: inspire consumers to go out and do interesting and extraordinary things. If Visa were the brand curating and inspiring consumers to achieve these experiences, then there was a good chance participants would be more prone to transact with Visa while doing them.

The premise of Go in Six was indeed designed and architected for the flick. By design, every piece of content Visa developed to tell its story contained no more than six words of copy, six seconds of video, or six images (refer to Figure 16.4 for a sample content piece). This "less is more" approach created a framework for Visa to tell stories in hyper short form, conveying powerful messages to the consumer before they were flicked down on the smartphone screen. Visa also invited consumers to join the conversation, prompting them to use Instagram to tell how they "Go."

By using a variety of third party data inputs, Visa inspired consumers to pursue contextually relevant experiences that could be achieved with Visa. Using historical data and geo-targeting, consumers on platforms like Facebook and Twitter were inspired to go crawfishing, participate in the Color Run, and other extraordinary

FIGURE 16.4   An example of the content from Visa'a Go in Six Campaign (Created by MRY)

activities that they might not have otherwise known about.

The stories Go in Six served up hit the bullseye in providing value and generating engagement and sharing. The sharing of Go in Six content led to an astonishing 330 million earned impressions over the course of the campaign, and engagement rates with campaign content were 10 times the industry standard. Prior to Go in Six, Visa was ranked #56 out of the top brands on Facebook according to tech platform Unmetric and #7 in the financial services category. After this campaign, Visa was the #2 social media brand overall and #1 in financial services. Storytelling done right indeed achieves rapid and astonishing results.[4]

Be inclusive: Starbucks

As brand stories are told, expect the crowd to chime in—sometimes positively, sometimes not. For better or for worse, though, one thing is for certain. IF the crowd cares enough about your story to listen, they will care enough to talk back. Your brand's ability to market with consumers instead of just at them will make your stories much more powerful and likely to be shared.

Starbucks has always been at the forefront of engaging consumers through the power of stories. In 2014 Starbucks launched a Global transmedia campaign called "Meet Me at Starbucks" to reinforce the value of its brand among a sea of competitors. Transmedia is a storytelling approach where a single story is narrated across multiple platforms. In the case of Meet Me at Starbucks, both traditional mediums like television and progressive platforms like Twitter were leveraged.

This campaign is centered on the simple story of a day in the life of Starbucks around the world. The execution of capturing this story though was anything but simple, filming in 28 countries with 39 local filmmakers, and all within a 24-hour window. The result of the footage captured fueled everything from a 60-second TV spot to a mini-documentary to hundreds of social media posts in local markets.

Not only is Starbucks being inclusive via this effort by featuring its customers in their films, but anyone can participate in the campaign. Using the hashtag #HowWeMet consumers can submit photos and stories of how they met on Twitter, some of which will add to the Starbucks campaign.

The Storytelling Mandate

By having a strong brand story, being known for one thing, being human, inspiring action, and being inclusive of your audience, the best brands in the world are using stories, and not advertising, to create meaningful engagement and a lasting impact on their audience. By flipping the approach from selling stuff to offering value, brands are adapting to the consumer-led disruption of consumer media.

Now more than ever, if you want your business to be heard, you need a story worth sharing that arrests today's flick-happy consumer to stop and enjoy your narrative. What will soon become apparent is that businesses and brands that do not evolve into this new form of communications may see themselves disappear as fast as a flick on a consumer's smartphone.

Epilogue

We live in an incredibly inspiring and hopeful time. Despite the persistent ongoing fears of economic uncertainty, terrorism, and increased global competition, the United States is still in the driver's seat just in a different, and perhaps more positive way. Unlike in generations past though where America was able to impose its will with brute force and strength, today in America our ability to persevere and succeed rests largely on our intuition and understanding of what lies ahead. Our imperative now is to deliver the innovations today that meet the needs of tomorrow.

It is within the relentless naivety of YouthNation that our greatest inventions and linchpins of global competitiveness are now being born. Google, Facebook, YouTube, and Twitter were all first conceived by young and inspired thinkers who were able to see what was next. Where would our nation be if we couldn't call these innovations our own?

Right now, there is no industry that is immune to the disruption posed by the forces of technology, automation, globalization, and big data. It is indeed YouthNation that is best setup to transform disruption into opportunity. The hardwiring of young brains during the digital era has forged a path for intuitive thinking that in some cases transcends the abilities of even the world's most powerful corporations.

Whether you are a new college graduate entering the workforce, a small business owner struggling to get ahead, or a Global CMO faced with maintaining the growth needed to prosper, every business needs to learn to manage the change occurring around your business, or it will undoubtedly manage you. If you have gotten to this point in the book it should be clear that we are now living in a different world. It is no longer top-down but bottom up. The world is being changed on the sidewalks more than in the boardrooms.

It is now more important than ever for we as business leaders to stay updated on the world around us. Believe it or not, even the most trivial trends being adopted by YouthNation can have a massive impact on your business, industry, and future. Keep an eye on popular technology and lifestyle blogs, use Twitter, talk to the young people around you and ask the hard questions to understand what is really happening.

You are indeed empowered, regardless of age, to take the imagination and reckless abandon of YouthNation and implement its way of thinking and core principles into your business. Youth can indeed be a state of mind—a state of mind that can be adopted by anyone who wants to take firm hold of the opportunities created by the technological advancement of our society and move boldly forward into the future.

What's Next?

America's cultural and business landscape will undoubt-edly evolve more in the next five years than it has in the past 50. This is inevitable. It is within this evolution where explosive opportunities will emerge and institu-tions will crumble. I believe that those organizations and individuals who adopt the principles of YouthNation will be best prepared to be on the right side of disruption. Here is what I believe the next five years holds for our YouthNation-driven society.

Physical retailers will crumble

Rising real estate costs in highly dense metropolitan areas will make the business of physically selling most durable goods to consumers unsustainable. Amazon's buying power, selection, data, speed, and technology will force retailers of everything from electronics, to clothing, to toiletries, to completely rethink their models. Most physi-cal retailers are already building sophisticated mobile apps to compete with Amazon. Luxury retailers will greatly diminish their square footage in affluent areas to further what they are already becoming: showrooms. If a retailer is not selling something a consumer needs within the hour then they will not be able to compete with Amazon who will have it there within an hour—for cheaper.

The TV and computer will become one

The age-old ritual of sitting in front of the TV after a long day will not change, but the TV itself will. TV will be fed content from the Internet and not from a cable feed. You will not turn to channels but press apps, which will bring up individual shows or content platforms like the NFL. Broadcast TV networks will either disappear or reinvent themselves as full-time studios. Advertising on TV will primarily address the "value consumer" as the luxury market will simply pay to not have to see commercials.

Coastal cities will continue to expand outward

As foreign investors continue to eye American real estate as a safe place to put their money, home prices in the heart of major cities will continue to skyrocket and be unattainable except for the uber-wealthy. Many cities on the innovation-heavy coasts will start to look like 5th Avenue in New York City with luxurious properties high above the city sitting empty as an investment instrument for overseas billionaires. This trend will continue to force YouthNation to expand their urban boundaries driving more and more gentrification. Our city's skyscrapers and cultural hubs will continue to expand outward changing the landscape of our nation.

The entrepreneur will go mainstream

The tools and opportunities brought about by the peer-to-peer economy will indeed allow more and more individuals with specialized skillsets to become entrepreneurial in their pursuit of financial independence. The traditional 9 to 5 work life will be replaced by a flexible more prosperous lifestyle for those whom have taken the necessary steps to create marketable skills in the new economy. Companies will respond by trimming their workforces, pensions, and overheads to become leaner in a world predicated on change as the only constant.

People will get married later and have less children

With travel getting cheaper, the costs of buying a home and educating children getting more expensive, and social media giving YouthNation endless opportunities, tools, and temptations to meet new people, the institution of marriage will continue to be pushed until later in life. Furthermore, as the divorce rate for the parents of YouthNation reach all-time highs there will be a pervasive fear in getting married at all. This may in fact result in less children being born and a relative ease on our population growth compared to prior generations.

Wealth disparity will accelerate

As technology continues to automate, more jobs will get offshored; and wealth disparity will continue to accelerate. The rich, with access to capital and techno-logical innovation will continue to get richer. The poor, looking from the outside in at societal advancements and shrinking labor opportunities, will unfortunately continue to get poorer. This will place a tremendous strain on our nation which will be forced to reevaluate everything from taxes, to infrastructure investments, to social security to ensure that we don't revert permanently to the economic make-up of the roaring twenties. It sounds far-fetched, but maybe not so much.

The Maker Movement will liberate the consumer

As 3-D printers (tools which allow consumers to print products like toothbrushes and picture frames) get cheaper and more readily accessible, the consumer will be able to manufacture their own everyday products, right in their own homes. Prototypes for durable goods will be shared online, and products we can't even imagine right now will be available for printing at the touch of a button. Our reliance on traditional retailers will wane and innovations for new products that make our lives easier and more affordable will be designed, shared, and printed everyday at will.

"Barbell economics" will rule the day

In a nation of wealth disparity, companies will need to make a finite choice between being a value play (Wal-Mart, Dollar Store, Vizio) or a luxury play (Apple, Mercedes, Coach). There simply won't be room for companies to play in the middle, as the middle class will continue to erode. The path to winning in corporate America will either be a race for who can be most efficient in creating serviceable products at the cheapest price (winning on supply chain and distribution innovation) or who can be the most groundbreaking in brand building and product innovation.

Education will become more specialized

Tech luminaries like Mark Zuckerberg and Bill Gates are behind Code.org, which is seeking to implement computer science classes in every K–12 school in the U.S. An argument can indeed be made that the language of code will be nearly as important as the language of English in 10 years. We are indeed moving into a workforce where the specialist, rather than the "jack of all trades, master of none" will be in demand.

Getting an MBA but lacking a marketable skill in a shaky corporate America seems like a far-flung strategy to pay down massive student loans. Education will need to become far more specialized far more quickly. The trade schools, seen as "down-market" will have the chance to reinvent themselves for a changing world that may indeed be devoid of middle management.

Renting will become the new buying

Experience-obsessed YouthNation will continue to question the notion of sinking core net worth into cars and houses. As Uber and Airbnb have proven, access will be more desirable than ownership in the future.

Facebook and Google (and perhaps Amazon and Apple) may all become too powerful and be broken up

As Facebook and Google continue to swallow up companies, collect more data, enter the commerce space, and start to control everything from home automation to the television, they will simply become too powerful and monopolistic for our economy to remain competitive. These new mega corporations could become a threat to the balance of our economy and will likely need to be broken apart.

Social will continue to go "dark"

It's not that YouthNation wants privacy from each other, just from the public. This is the distinction, which will transform the very fabric of social media from being a public and open platform to being one that is both ephemeral and anonymous. Emerging platforms like Snapchat, YikYak, Whisper, and Secret are in many ways the anti-Facebook, protecting users from the long-term consequences of their sharing and dialogue while still providing real-time social connectivity. This will provide a real challenge for brands that will struggle to find an effective strategy on platforms where they have no functional role.

One device

Apple's iPhone 6 proved to the marketplace that at the right size a phone really does replace the need for an iPad or other tablet. With that in mind and the role of the desktop continuing to dramatically shrink outside of the workplace, YouthNation will be primarily moving to a one-device lifestyle with the smartphone at the center. This will shift brands looking to reach consumers from a "mobile first" strategy to a "mobile only" strategy.

All content, whether entertainment, work, or personal, will be accessed from the smartphone, via the cloud. Using technologies like Apple's AirPlay, content will be wirelessly beamed to flat screen displays, wearables, and other accessories. YouthNation is always in motion and they cannot be weighed down with anything that isn't absolutely necessary.

Internet everywhere

The Internet of Things will transform products on the road, home, and office. Nearly every appliance or product will begin to speak to the Internet. Your refrigerator will tell Amazon that you've run out of eggs; your thermostat will automatically adjust based on weather patterns (see Google's acquisition of Nest); your car will begin to speak to the mechanic when it is having problems. This means that now nearly every company needs to become a technology company. Old world manufacturers will need to get smarter in order to meet the progressive needs of YouthNation.

Conclusion

I feel so privileged to have spent the first 20 years of my career working closely with the future of this great nation. To think of the changes that I have seen before my very eyes since starting in business can be quite startling at times. What is certain is that the evolution to American culture, society, and business is only going to accelerate. Another certainty is that these changes are going to be almost always initiated in some form by YouthNation.

It can be easy to write off someone with less experience than you. But sometimes, experience can be overrated. We have a habit of becoming jaded and single-minded through our experiences. It can limit our minds to dream up what is possible. The reality though is that today's technological innovations are redefining what is possible, and all our lives are being redefined as well.

I hope this book has inspired you to reimagine your future. I hope this book has opened your eyes to the world changing around you. Lastly I hope this book has empowered you to embrace the disruptive societal forces at play and harness them as a force for good in your life and in your career.

Endnotes

Foreword

1. http://www.dazeinfo.com/2014/01/23/smartphone
-users-growth-mobile-internet-2014-2017/

Chapter 3: The Rise of Electronic Dance Music

1. California Hotel Service, about Coachella
(www.californiahotelservice.com)
2. About Burning Man (www.burningman.com)
3. California Hotel Service/Indio, California
(www.californiahotelservice.com)

Chapter 4: Access over Ownership

1. Emily Badger, "Why Plummeting Millennial
Homeownership Isn't as Alarming as It Seems"
Wonkblog, 2014 (http://www.washingtonpost.com

/blogs/wonkblog/wp/2014/07/16/why-plummeting
-millennial-homeownership-isnt-as-alarming-as-it
-seems/)

2. Rick Newman, "The Real Reason Millennials Don't
   Buy Cars and Homes" The Exchange, 2013
   (http://finance.yahoo.com/blogs/the-exchange
   /real-reason-millennials-don-t-buy-cars-homes
   -153340750.html)

3. Airbnb About page (https://www.airbnb.com/
   about/about-us)

4. Rick Rouan, "Uber, Lyft Taking a Bite out of Taxis"
   The Columbus Dispatch, 2014 (http://www.dispatch
   .com/content/stories/local/2014/10/13/uber-lyft-
   taking-bite-out-of-taxi-business.html)

Chapter 5: The Communal Table

1. Lauren Weber, "Companies Say Goodbye to the
   'Burbs" Wall Street Journal, 2013
   (http://ny.curbed.com/archives/2014/01/06/10_year
   _study_shows_huge_price_jumps_across_brooklyn
   .php)

2. Jefferson Graham, "It's Hip to Be Tech in Brooklyn's
   Dumbo" USA Today, 2013
   (http://www.usatoday.com/story/tech/columnist
   /talkingtech/2013/05/02/new-york-tech-startup
   -scene/2127385/)

3. "EPA Finalizes Cleanup Plan for Gowanus Canal
   Superfund Site in Brooklyn, New York; $506 Million

Cleanup Will Remove Contaminated Sediment and Create Jobs" EPA press release, 2013 (http://yosemite.epa.gov/opa/admpress.nsf /0/B1CF5011D9857EA585257BF6005286D5)

4. "Gowanus Open Studios 2014" South Brooklyn Network press release, 2014 (http://www .southbrooklyn.com/news-and-stories/gowanus/ gowanus-open-studios-2014-gos-2014)

5. Laura Kusisto, "Gowanus Passes Sniff Test for Some Start Ups" Wall Street Journal, 2014 (http://online.wsj.com/articles/gowanus-passes-sniff -test-for-some-startups-1406683589)

Chapter 6: The Peer-to-Peer Economy

1. Amy Kamenetz, "Why the Sharing Economy is Growing" Fast Company Magazine, 2013 (http://www.fastcoexist.com/1682080/why-the -sharing-economy-is-growing)

2. Elliot Martin and Susan Shaheen, "The Impact of Carsharing on Household Vehicle Ownership" Access, The Magazine of UCTC, 2011 (http://www.uctc.net/access/38/access38_carsharing _ownership.shtml)

3. Jordan Crook, "Meetup.com Surpasses 100 Million RSVP's to 10 Million Meetups" Tech Crunch, 2013 (http://techcrunch.com/2013/05/28/meetup-com -surpasses-100-million-rsvps-to-10-million -meetups/)

4. Meetup.com About page (www.meetup.com)

Chapter 7: The Power of the Crowd

1. Dan L., "Crash the Superbowl Ad Meter Results" Video Content News, 2011 (http://videocontestnews .com/2011/02/07/2011-crash-the-super-bowl-ad-meter-results/)
2. Liz Stinson, "How GE Plans to Act Like a Start Up and Crowdsource Great Ideas" Wired Magazine, 2014 (http://www.wired.com/2014/04/how-ge-plans-to-act-like-a-startup-and-crowdsource-great-ideas/)
3. Kickstarter Help page (https://www.kickstarter.com/help/stats)

Chapter 8: Free Agency

1. Mitra Toosi, "Employment Outlook: 2010–2020 Labor Force Projections to 2020: A More Slowly Growing Workforce" Monthly Labor Review, 2012 (http://www.bls.gov/opub/mlr/2012/01/art3full.pdf)
2. "The Disappearing Defined Benefit Pension and Its Potential Impact on the Retirement Incomes of Baby Boomers" Social Security Bulletin, 2009 (http://www.ssa.gov/policy/docs/ssb/v69n3/v69n3p1 .html)
3. Elise Gould, "Public Insurance Is Increasingly Crucial to American Families Even as Employer-Sponsored Health Insurance Coverage Ends Its Steady Decline" Economic Policy Institute, 2013 (http://www.epi.org/publication/employer

-sponsored-health-insurance-is-still-failing
-american-families/)

4. Sara Horowitz and Fabio Rosati, "53 Million
   Americans Are Freelancing" Freelancer's Union
   2014 Survey (https://www.freelancersunion
   .org/blog/dispatches/2014/09/04/53million/)

5. Deep Nishar, "The Next Three Billion" LinkedIn
   blog, 2014 (http://blog.linkedin.com/2014/04/18/
   the-next-three-billion/)

6. Laura Shin, "How to Use LinkedIn, 5 Smart Steps"
   Forbes Magazine, 2014 (http://www.forbes.com/
   sites/laurashin/2014/06/26/how-to-use-linkedin-
   5-smart-steps-to-career-success/)

7. Taskrabbit How it works page
   (https://www.taskrabbit.com/how-it-works)

8. Michael Carney, "The Gig Economy Is Growing
   Up" Pando Daily, 2013 (http://pando.com/2013/
   12/18/the-gig-economy-is-growing-up-elance-
   and-odesk-just-merged-to-dominate-it/)

9. Alex Farcet, "David Cohen Founder of Tech Stars"
   Starupbootcamp.dk, 2009
   (https://www.youtube.com/watch?v=8i80uXcMq1g)

Chapter 9: Lifehacking

1. Rebecca Ungarino, "Burdened with Record Amount
   of Debt, Graduates Delay Marriage" NBC News,
   2014 (http://www.nbcnews.com/business/personal-

finance/burdened-record-amount-debt-graduates-delay-marriage-n219371)

2. Alyson Shontell, "General Assembly Has Had 6,000 People Take Its Classes, and It's Opening a Second Huge Campus in NYC" Business Insider, 2013 (http://www.businessinsider.com/general-assembly -915-broadway-campus-2012-1#ixzz3MNI6sBaphttp://www.businessinsider.com/general-assembly-915 -broadway-campus-2012-1)

3. Profile of CrowdTap on Inc.com (http://www.inc.com/profile/crowdtap)

Chapter 11: The End of Demographics

1. James B. Stewart, "A 21st Century Fox Time Warner Merger Would Narrow Already Dwindling Competition" New York Times, 2014 (http://www .nytimes.com/2014/07/26/business/a-21st -century-fox-time-warner-merger-would-narrow -already-dwindling-competition.html)

2. "Super Bowl XLVII Draws 111.5 Million Viewers, 25.3 Million Tweets" Nielsen Newswire, 2014 (http://www.nielsen.com/us/en/insights/news/2014 /super-bowl-xlviii-draws-111-5-million-viewers-25-3 -million-tweets.html)

3. Daniel Frankel, "Millennials Time Shift Nearly Half Their Programming Study Says" Fire Cable, 2014 (http://www.fiercecable.com/story/millennials-time -shift-nearly-half-their-programming-study-says /2014-10-14)

4. NFL on Fox press release
   (http://tvbythenumbers.zap2it.com/2014/08/06/nfl
   -on-fox-stacks-broadcast-teams-with-new-familiar
   -faces-for-20th-anniversary-season/290866/)

Chapter 14: People Are Brands

1. Victor Luckerson, "5 Reasons Disney Will Pay up to
   950 Million to Be On YouTube" Time Magazine,
   2014 (http://time.com/37256/why-disney-is-
   buying-maker-studios/)

Chapter 16: A Story Worth Sharing

1. Douglas MacMillan, Evelyn M. Rusli, "Snapchat Is
   Said to Have More than 100 Million Monthly Active
   Users" Digits, Tech News and Analysis from the
   WSJ, 2014 (http://blogs.wsj.com/digits/2014/
   08/26/snapchat-said-to-have-more-than-100-
   million-monthly-active-users/)

2. Evelyn M. Rusli and Douglas MacMillan, "Snapchat
   Spurned $3 Billion Acquisition Offer from Facebook"
   Digits, Tech News and Analysis from the WSJ, 2013
   (http://blogs.wsj.com/digits/2013/11/13/snapchat
   -spurned-3-billion-acquisition-offer-from-facebook/)

3. Catherine Clifford, "Millennials Check Their Phones
   43 Times a Day. This Is What They're Looking For"
   Entrepreneur Magazine, 2014 (http://www.
   entrepreneur.com/article/234531)

4. Russell Cooke, "Go Big or Go Pro" Business to Community, 2014 (www.business2community .com/content-marketing/go-big-gopro-gopro-marketing-strategy-defines-content-marketing-01055894)

Index

Page references followed by *fig* indicate an illustrated figure; followed by *t* indicate a table.